Sports Law and Litigation

Sports Law and Litigation

Craig Moore
LLB (London)
Barrister
Barnards Inn Chambers, London

CLT Professional Publishing
A Division of Central Law Training Ltd

© Craig Moore 1997

Published by
CLT Professional Publishing
A division of Central Law Training Ltd
Wrens Court
52-54 Victoria Road
Sutton Coldfield
Birmingham B72 1SX

ISBN 1 85811 161 7

Produced by Palladian, PO Box 15, Bembridge
Typeset by Cheryl Zimmerman
Printed in Great Britain by Redwood Books Ltd

*To my parents
for their love and support*

Contents

Summary of Contents

Preface

This book attempts to show the legal practitioner who works at the coalface of the law how its undeniable, and increasingly close, relationship with sport operates, and to assist in achieving a greater understanding of the subject. It is intended to be a practical work of first reference for full-time litigators, as well as those who might, only once in their career, be called upon to advise an Eric Cantona, a Diane Modhal, or a Jean-Marc Bosman. The book has a bias towards personal injury-related issues since such claims are likely to be encountered by most practitioners on a day-to-day basis. Recent developments in the courts, coupled with a greater awareness of legal rights, means that the practice of advising clients who suffer injuries whilst participating in sporting activities is likely to increase and, in that regard, a thorough knowledge of the relevant legal issues will be required by practitioners. That knowledge is also, of course, an essential prerequisite for those who advise and represent sports clubs, associations and other bodies, including local authorities etc. The status of clubs and other sporting bodies is touched upon in this book, as are the related subjects of taxation, value added tax, and intellectual property. However, those subjects are the province of more specialist works and no attempt is made to address them in any detail here.

Writing a book is often a lonely furrow to plough and I have nothing but admiration for those who regularly produce far weightier tomes than this. I would like to thank my colleagues and friends for their advice and encouragement, and Central Law Training for giving me the opportunity to write on a subject for which I have a genuine passion. I am also grateful to my colleagues at Barnards Inn Chambers for proof reading each of the chapters as they evolved, invariably to hit the cutting-room floor as recommendations were made (although I hasten to add that any errors are mine!). I recently attended the inaugural meeting of the Bar Sports Law Group where the constitution of the Group was discussed. That brief debate made me realise that there will inevitably be those who will disagree with the views expressed by me in this book. If so, good. Conflicting opinions are the essence of the law, just as healthy competition is the life and soul of sport. I fervently hope that in some small way I am able to encourage discussion which will assist in taking our understanding of the subject to a higher level. Ultimately, sport touches most of our lives to a greater or lesser extent and if, like the author, the reader actually takes a keen interest in sport, it will, I hope, make the task of achieving a competent grasp of the synthesis between the law and sport that much easier.

Craig Moore
Barnards Inn Chambers
Trinity Day 1997

Table of Cases

Table of Statutes

Table of Rules and Orders

Introduction

"If all the year were playing holidays,
To sport would be as tedious as to work"
(Shakespeare, *Henry IV, Part I*)

Historical background

In medieval times, Shrove Tuesday was the day which preceded the long fast of Lent and was marked by feasts and other merriment which, in some towns and villages, included lawless and uncontrolled games of "football" played over vast areas. The game has survived in Ashbourne, Derbyshire, where the two sides, the Up'ards and Down'ards, live on opposite sides of Henmore Brook, which runs through the middle of the town. The goals are mill spindles which are three miles apart and to score a goal the ball has to be touched against the spindle three times. There is no limit to the number of participants and the game is a giant free-for-all, known locally as the "hug". Games can last for as long as eight hours and, not infrequently, limbs are broken. Such occurrences are regarded as an occupational hazard by the many thousands who have taken part in the game over the centuries. The rudimentary rules of the game and complete lack of regulation are still "observed" today in deference to the history and pageant of the game. Over the years, no one has ever suggested that the rules of the game be changed to conform with socially acceptable standards of behaviour prevailing at the relevant time. Yet it is inconceivable that such an event could have endured in modern times as anything other than an annual piece of theatre, without major intervention by either the rule-makers or the courts. The game has survived unchanged (and unspoiled?) simply because it is an historical anachronism which those who take part in have no desire to alter.

Several hundred years after the elementary games of Medieval Europe were first played, the roots of many sports can be found on the playing-fields of the public schools of Victorian England. The laws of association football, rugby union and cricket all developed at a time when simply playing those games was an end in itself, and notions of fair play were more pure and far less susceptible to outside influences than they are today. The increasing commercialism in sport, culminating in the pivotal role which it now enjoys, means that many modern games are driven principally by financial considerations, sometimes to the detriment of the ideals which the originators of sport contemplated. The politicisation of sport has also been responsible, in no small measure, for undermining the tenets which underpinned sport in its infancy – a blatant example being Adolf Hitler's barely disguised agenda in the staging of the 1936 Olympic Games in Berlin (only to be spectacularly upstaged by the US athlete Jesse Owens). The black power salute given by Lee Evans and other US athletes on the podium at the Mexico Olympics also lingers in the memory, as does the murder of Israeli athletes at the Games in Munich.

As the finishing touches were being put to these pages, the Grand National was cynically hijacked by terrorists for their own political ends, depriving a worldwide audience of 350 million of their enjoyment of the most famous steeplechase. The perpetrators were clearly mindful of the exposure which their shameless act was capable of achieving, and it underlines the simultaneous power and vulnerability of sport. As the barrister, Edward Grayson, observes in the second edition of his book *Sport and the Law*, if one couples those factors with the twin evils of violence and drugs, and the corrupting influence they have all had on sport, it is little wonder that the playing-field of today is very different to the one of a century or so ago. Having said that, such adverse influences have coincided with positive developments, not least of which is the fact that the barriers of many sports have broken down to enable them to be enjoyed across the social spectrum. The influx of money has also provided massive financial benefits for sport. Who can seriously argue that the standard and standing of English football has not improved immeasurably since the huge financial injection by Sky TV, or that there has not been a quantum leap in the standard of our stadia in the first half of this decade? The Corinthian values observed by the Gentlemen and Players may be a distant memory, but there is a danger of looking at sport through rose-coloured spectacles. The playing-field has undoubtedly changed, but it is still essentially level for those who abide by the rules. Moreover, the fact that the Grand National was able to take place two days later than scheduled shows that sport can gloriously prevail over adversity.

What is "sport"?

There is no recognised definition of "sport", and it is generally accepted that the word is more susceptible to description than definition. Given that basic difficulty, it ought logically to follow that the concept of "sports law" is similarly incapable of any meaningful definition. Moreover, the first and foremost point to note is that there is no magic to the convenient shorthand term "sports law" which covers such a diverse range of disciplines as crime, contract, tort, employment law, taxation and copyright. The reality is that the courts have been called upon to rule upon sports-related litigation since the nineteenth century and, whilst the tentacles of the law have reached out and taken a firm grip on the world of sport through both legislation and precedent, it would be wrong to say that there is a self-compartmentalised body of so-called "sports law". The title of this book should therefore be regarded as no more than a convenient handle. Nevertheless, in certain respects, the law relating to sporting activities is clearly distinguishable from its application in other social contexts, as will be shown. Parliament has also passed legislation which is specifically intended to eradicate the evil of crowd trouble at sporting events, and to address the well-documented failure of organisers of such events to protect the safety of the legitimate spectator.

Perhaps the more pertinent question, and one to which a satisfactory answer capable of universal application has not yet been formulated, is: what is "lawful sport"? Any attempt at answering that difficult question must involve an examination of how the Rule of Law applies to the many and varied conflicts arising in the sporting arena. In other words, how do the laws of individual sports recognise the fundamental distinction between right and wrong which lies at the heart of any jurisprudential debate? The Rule of Law is conspicuous by its absence in a recent attempt to define "sport" in the 1993 European Sports Charter, where sport is said to include:

> "... all forms of physical activity which through casual or organised participation aim at expressing and improving physical fitness and mental well-being, forming social relationships or obtaining results in competition levels."

Sport, like society generally, is developing and evolving constantly just as society is, and probably the best that can be done is to identify the elements which ought to be present in a legitimate sporting activity without putting them into any form of words which purports to be a definitive response to the question "what is sport?". Those elements include: physical activity, health, education, social interaction, competition, and the Rule of Law. No precedence is intended by placing them in that order, although the Rule of Law clearly must underpin the other elements.

Relationship between sport and the law

The relationship between sport and the law is a subject which has only captured the imagination of lawyers and those involved in sport in relatively recent times. With sports personalities being elevated to the status of demi-gods, and seemingly limitless exposure for sport as a consequence of media attention with the attendant financial rewards for all concerned, it is not surprising that the law has taken an ever-increasing interest in sport. It is true to say that such intrusion has not been universally welcomed by the administrators of sport, who jealously guard their ability to manage their own affairs. However, the sophisticated society in which we live means that the law is now an essential tool (many would say a necessary evil) in those areas of life which, in an ideal world, we would prefer to remain as unencumbered as possible. Whilst the courts have shown a marked reluctance to interfere when the judicial review machinery has been invoked, the injunction granted to a player in *Jones and another* v *Welsh Rugby Football Union* (1997) *The Times*, 6 March indicates a willingness on the part of courts to become involved in disciplinary procedures which were previously regarded as the exclusive preserve of sporting bodies.

The other factor which has fuelled the law's increasing involvement in sport is the seemingly insatiable appetite of the public – fed by an obliging media. Whether this is any indication of the interest which society at large takes in sport and the law is debatable, but the relationship is now firmly entrenched and likely to increase in its intensity. The recent case of *Smoldon* v *Whitworth & Nolan* (1996) *The Times*, 18 December (CA) underlines the developing nature of the relationship, and also demonstrates the enormous interest created by sports-related litigation – even those cases which do not involve high-profile parties. During the relatively short course of writing this book, a number of decisions made by the courts in sports-related cases were described as "landmark", most notably a judicial finding to the effect that a professional footballer's career had been ended by a negligent tackle (see Chapter 5, "Civil Liability On and Off the Field of Play"). "Landmark" is a word that journalists are apt to use a little freely on occasions, but the inescapable fact is that sport now plays such an important part in so many people's lives – in the case of a privileged few, a fundamental part – that it is bound to give rise to disputes which, like the games themselves, attract intense debate and scrutiny.

Chapter 1

Government of Sport

Introduction

If the word "government" is interpreted in its broadest sense to include regulation and control, it is possible to discern a hierarchy from central government at the top, to referees and other officials at the bottom, with the various governing bodies of sport and the courts somewhere in between. However, this hierarchy ignores the fact that the first and foremost layer of government must come from within sport itself, since it is the administrators who bear the initial responsibility for formulating rules and regulations which respect the Rule of Law, and for then ensuring that they are enforced. In order to achieve these twin objectives, it is clearly essential that those who are subject to the rules and regulations must have respect for them. The relationship between a governing body and its members (whether they are clubs or individuals) is founded on a contract, either formal or informal, that the members will abide by the rules and be subject to certain sanctions if they transgress. Invariably, some kind of consideration will pass from each side to make the arrangement legally binding. At the very least, a relationship of mutual trust and confidence must exist for things to work. However, it is doubtful whether the participants themselves ever stop to think about the precise reason why they abide by the rules of their sport, accepting fines and bans when they are handed out; they simply do – at least in the vast majority of cases.

The reason why sport in this country has been able, for the most part, to conduct its own affairs without outside intervention probably lies in its innate capacity for self-regulation and administration, from grass roots to the very highest levels. The modern day machinery which exists for the regulation of horse racing and cricket can be traced back to the eighteenth century, when both the Jockey Club and the MCC were founded. The Football Association (FA) has existed for over a century. It would be surprising, therefore, if these governing bodies had not, by the late 1990s, developed sophisticated administrative, regulatory and disciplinary procedures. However, within a particular sport, clubs and individuals may be affiliated to a number of different bodies by whose rules and regulations they agree to abide. This can create difficulties where more than one of the administrative bodies has power to impose sanctions for the same offence and the individual or club is thus exposed to double jeopardy. For instance, a professional footballer who contracts to transfer to one club and then signs for another, may find himself on the receiving end of punishment from the FA, UEFA and FIFA, not to mention the courts, which may be called upon to resolve the implications of the player's breach of contract.

Moreover, at present, one of the principal issues facing sport's governing bodies is how to implement effective and binding disciplinary procedures which will prevent a flood of claims being pursued through the courts. If that issue is not urgently addressed, there is a real danger that the demarcation lines between sport's internal disciplinary committees and the courtroom will break down irretrievably. Neither sport, not the courts, could cope if every aggrieved party resorted to law. The Court of Arbitration for Sport (CAS), set up by the International Olympic Committee (IOC) in 1983, is perhaps the best example of how sport has acted in an attempt to ensure that its disputes are resolved internally and not exposed to the glare of publicity in the courts. An Independent Arbitration Panel, modelled along the lines of the CAS, has just been proposed in this country by the Central Council for Physical Recreation (CCPR) (see the *Independent*, 8 April 1997). How such a body would be able to keep compensation claims, as opposed to disciplinary disputes, out of the courts is unclear. Additionally, experience shows that at whatever level disciplinary issues are resolved, the assistance of lawyers is a necessary evil; the ad hoc committee of the CAS, which was set up specifically for the Atlanta Olympics, included a glittering array of legal talent.

This chapter deals with the role which central government plays in sport, and outlines the relationship between sport and the courts, a union of which the administrators of sport clearly disapprove. However, in a society which is all too ready to resort to litigation, and with the huge financial rewards available in professional sport, it seems inevitable that sport will enter the courtroom increasingly.

The role of central government

Successive governments have kept sport afloat, but no more than that. The profile of sport at central government level has often depended as much on the energy and enthusiasm of the minister responsible, as the needs of sport itself. The last but one Labour Minister for Sport, Dennis Howell (now Lord Howell), is reckoned by many commentators to have made one of the greatest contributions to raising the priority given to sport. The importance of physical education was recognised in the years between (and during) the two world wars by the Education Acts of 1918 and 1944, by the creation, in 1925, of the National Playing Fields Association, and, in 1935, by the forerunner to the CCPR (under the auspices of the old Board of Education), both of which were dependent, initially, on funding from private sources. The (self) interest of central government in sport in the post-war years has principally been through fiscal measures which have tapped into the rich vein of revenue produced by sport. That interest apart, sports policy has, for many years, been the Cinderella of central government policy, with one or two notable exceptions such as the creation of the Sports Council in 1972 with an initial £3 million injection of government monies.

Bodies such as the Sports Council have, at least, had the advantage of devoting their attentions exclusively to the needs of sport and physical recreation, a distinction which cannot be awarded to the instruments of central government itself. Prior to the creation of the Department of National Heritage, responsibility for sports policy-making was spread across a number of governmental departments. Indeed, for some time, a tradition was established whereby the Minister for Sport would have concurrent responsibilities at the Department of the Environment (a bizarre situation which could have meant that the Sports Minister was also responsible for the nation's sewage works). The Cinderella effect has been ameliorated to some extent by the establishment of the Department of National Heritage and the funds which have become available for sport through the Sports Lottery Fund. Nevertheless, the range of central government departments retaining an interest in sport is bewildering. From the Foreign and Commonwealth Office, which can influence the staging of international events, to the Home Office, and HM Customs and Excise, almost every corner of government is, or could be, involved in sport. Perhaps more than any other, it is the omniscient presence of the Treasury which casts a lengthy shadow over every request for funding made by sport.

For many, the nadir of sport, in terms of the importance attached to it by central government, were the Thatcher years. During the period from May 1979 until November 1991, no Parliamentary debates were initiated by the Government front bench on sports policy, with the exception of debates on isolated tragedies like Bradford and Hillsborough, or "moral panic" measures such as the Football Spectators Act 1989. The ill-fated identity card proposals represented the highwater mark, for many, of the Thatcher Government's failure to understand sport or to appreciate its importance in both a social and economic context. During the 12-year period, there were five different Ministers for Sport. The perceived apathy culminated, in November 1991, in an opposition motion attacking the neglect of sport by the Government (see *Hansard* (HC) Vol 199, cols 973-1018: 27 November 1991). Despite the enthusiasm for, and enjoyment of, sport shown by the former Prime Minister, John Major, the lamentable performance of the Great Britain team at the Atlanta Olympics underlined the fact that we have, if anything, regressed as a sporting nation, in terms of endeavour, in the post-Thatcher era. In the immediate aftermath of the 1996 Olympic Games, there was considerable debate concerning the malaise of British athletics and the measures which need to be taken to put matters right. However, that debate seems to have evaporated as quickly as it formed.

On the positive side, the Sports Lottery Fund has already provided a much needed financial boost and will continue to do so. In addition, improvements in crowd behaviour at football matches and in ground safety in this country are due, in no small measure, to central government initiatives rather than any measures from within the game itself.

Department of National Heritage

Minister for Sport

The newly appointed Minister for Sport, Tony Banks MP, is a Parliamentary Under-Secretary at the Department of National Heritage. He is ultimately responsible to the Secretary of State for National Heritage, Chris Smith MP, whose brief tenure in office has already been marked by a clash with the directors of Camelot, the company responsible for running the National Lottery over proposed salary rises. The portfolio of the Parliamentary Under-Secretary is broad, ranging from the arts, broadcasting and the press, to museums, galleries, heritage and tourism. In 1996, that workload was shared by 1,040 staff, compared with 4,720 staff in the Health Department and 11,370 in the Lord Chancellor' Department. It is not surprising, therefore, that the proportion of ministerial time devoted to sport is relatively small. Furthermore, the Department of National Heritage does not have control over all aspects of sport and physical recreation. For example, responsibility for the teaching of games in schools – a critical aspect of the development of successful individuals and teams – rests with the Department of Employment and Education.

Arts, Sports and Lottery Group

The Arts, Sports and Lottery Group is divided into four subdivisions. The Sport and Recreation Division, headed by a Grade 5 civil servant, is responsible for policy on the visual and performing arts, sport and active recreation, and the National Lottery. It sponsors the Arts Council for England, the Crafts Council, the Sports Council and the Millenium Commission. It also supervises local authority and private funding of sport, and is responsible for business sponsorship schemes for both sport and the arts. The hierarchical nature within the Department of National Heritage (DNH) is emphasised by the fact that the Sport and Recreation Division is, itself, subdivided into four further subdivisions, each headed by a high-ranking civil servant. Their functions can be summarised as follows:

- SARD A: sponsorship of the Sports Council and restructuring of the Council; British Sports Forum/CCPR issues; honours; regional sports councils; the National Lottery.
- SARD B: sporting performance and excellence; sport for young people and those with a disability; international matters, including drug abuse in sport; children's play and playground safety; water sports safety.
- SARD C: sports sponsorship; the Sportsmatch scheme; Foundation for Sport and the Arts; taxation; safety of sports grounds; football policy; the Football Licensing Authority; the Football Trust.
- SARD D: participation issues; countryside and water recreation; local authority expenditure; playing-fields; compulsory competitive tendering (CCT); sport in inner cities; swimming pool and leisure centre bye-laws.

Other groups within the DNH include the Broadcasting and Media Group which, as the name suggests, is responsible for sports broadcasting. The finance division of the Resources and Services Group is closely involved with any project requiring public expenditure. It also participated in the consultative process which led to the Law Commission's recent report *Consent in the Criminal Law*, and the proposed creation of a sports recognition body (see Chapter 4, "Crime on the Field of Play").

Sports Council

The Sports Council is an independent body funded by central government and was established by Royal Charter in 1972. The Council is responsible for developing sport and physical recreation and for liaising with international organisations to further the interests of British sport. To that end, the Council administers six national centres for sporting excellence, the best known being Lilleshall in Shropshire. It is also responsible for distributing the funds from the National Lottery to sport in England. Those functions are overseen by a committee of 10 members: an independent chairman, the chairmen of the four home country sports councils, one representative from each of the British Olympic Association, an amateur non-Olympic sport, and of professional sport. The two other members are independent, with strong sporting credentials (one from a professional and one from an amateur sporting background). The importance of the Sports Council was recognised by the Law Commission's recommendation that the Council should be responsible for conferring recognition on lawful sports.

Sports Lottery Fund

The Sports Lottery Fund is administered by the National Lottery Division within the DNH, although money for capital projects is actually distributed by the Sports Council. In the two years since its inception, the Fund has distributed in the region of £500 million to some 2,000 sporting projects. Any sports club or organisation can apply for a grant, but each applicant must provide partnership funding and contribute towards the overall cost of the particular project. Once an application has been approved, a case officer is appointed who assists in the organisation and administration of fund-raising. Early indications are that the case officer is instrumental in steering projects towards a satisfactory conclusion. It is also proposed that Lottery money will be used to fund British competitors preparing for the next Olympic Games in Sydney.

Relationship between sport and the law

It has already been noted that, in the first instance, the task of ensuring acceptable standards of play, and policing the conduct of participants in accordance with the Rule of Law, lies in the hands of the various sporting bodies and associations which run sport. In a well-structured organisation, this takes place at three different levels:

(1) the formulation of the rules of the game which, amongst other things, ought expressly to forbid unfair and foul play;

(2) the application of immediate sanctions during the course of the game following a breach of the rules (*e.g.* booking or sending a player off); and

(3) the establishment of effective administrative machinery, including a disciplinary procedure, to ensure that those who break the rules are properly punished, and to enable those aggrieved by decisions to seek redress.

In most instances, there will be no separation of powers in the constitutional sense as the governing body will be acting as both law-maker and enforcer. There will be instances where the rules and/or sanctions provided for by a sport's governing body are inadequate. Alternatively, the body in question might decline, or fail, to take action against a participant where it is alleged that the rules of the sport have been contravened. Failing to take action where the rules have clearly been broken is a charge frequently levelled at football's governing bodies. Furthermore, where a player suffers damage or injury in the course of sport, and a dispute arises as to whether the injury was inflicted negligently or in breach of contract, the internal machinery of sport is not competent to try such claims, or to make legally enforceable awards of damages. In those situations, the aggrieved party will have to take his case to the next level, which, at present, means an action in the civil and/or criminal courts. At that point, the judge and jury become the arbiters of the rules of sport and assume the role of *quasi*-referee.

It would be contrary to public policy for the rules of a particular sport to purport to oust the jurisdiction of the courts, but if the parties to an agreement freely give their unfettered consent to refer a dispute to arbitration, it is doubtful whether either party could then seek to go behind such an agreement (for a discussion of the conditions of entry to the 1996 Olympic Games in Atlanta, see the section in Chapter 9, "Agreements Conferring Exclusive Jurisdiction"). In the case of an alleged assault during a football match, a prosecution may be brought by the Crown Prosecution Service even if action has been taken by the sporting body in question and/or the player's club. Similarly, the victim of alleged foul play has the option of instituting a private prosecution for assault or, the more likely course, a civil claim for trespass to the person. Those possibilities underline the point that if a player transgresses both the rules of his chosen sport, and the criminal law, he may be subjected to sanctions from a number of different sources, and whilst it may be relevant in mitigation, it will not provide him with a defence to say "I have already been punished". In public law, attempts to challenge the administrative actions of sport's governing bodies by way of judicial review proceedings have proved unsuccessful (see also Chapter 9). However, as will shortly be shown, the courts have been prepared to interfere in cases where privity of contract exists between the parties (*i.e.* in private law).

Challenging decisions made from "wet and windy" touchlines

On 27 February 1997 Ebsworth J granted Mark Jones, the Welsh international rugby player, an injunction lifting a suspension imposed by the Welsh Rugby Union for fighting during a match, until his appeal was heard (see *Jones and another* v *Welsh Rugby Football Union* (1997) *The Times*, 6 March). The case represents a significant development in the intervention by the courts in disciplinary sanctions imposed by sporting bodies. Jones was sent off whilst playing for his club, Ebbw Vale, after a fight with an opponent during a game against Swansea. He claimed that the four-week suspension imposed by the Welsh RU's disciplinary committee was unfair. He suffered from a bad stammer and said that that handicap prevented him from putting his case effectively. Additionally, the committee's rules did not allow for legal representation, the questioning of evidence, or the playing of the match video before the hearing.

Ebsworth J observed that for many years sporting decisions had been made from "wet and windy" touchlines, but the modern professional game meant that such rulings now affected many people who earned their living from the game. The judge said that Jones had been given "no real rights" and that the punishment was of "unreasonable length". Crucially, she said that it was "naive" to argue that the decisions of disciplinary committees could not be challenged in court because the sanctions imposed now had economic results on those affected. Jones earned £29,000 a year, but was able to earn bonuses of up to £10,000 for winning key games. However, those bonuses were forfeited when he was suspended. Ebsworth J said that since a player had to be registered with the Welsh RU and was subject to its disciplinary code, there was a form of contract between the two. She urged the committee to settle the case internally, which suggests a lingering reluctance on the part of the judiciary to rule on such disputes if possible.

Not surprisingly, reaction to the case has been mixed. Supporters of the decision argue that it will make disciplinary committees more accountable by recognising that there is a legal contract between a player and his sporting body, and that it takes account of the financial damage caused by suspension. Amongst the detractors, the Labour Party's sports spokesman at the time, Tom Hendry, said that the case set "a very damaging precedent". The English Cricket Board and the Football Association appeared unruffled by the decision, claiming that their respective disciplinary procedures were tried and tested methods of dealing with players who transgressed. A spokesman for the FA claimed that its disciplinary commissions were recognised as having the status of domestic tribunals and were respected by the law. Clearly, Ebsworth J thought otherwise about the disciplinary procedures adopted by the Welsh RU.

Jones' solicitor, who said "This is the first time, as far as we are aware, that there has been a successful challenge in the courts to the rules of a sporting body", appears to have overlooked the fact that in 1984 the High Court lifted a lifetime ban imposed on the judo wrestler Ron Angus for an alleged doping offence. It was accepted that a breach of the rules of natural justice had occurred at the hearing at which the ban was imposed. Angus' ban was lifted by the consent of the parties and so, presumably, the court was not called upon to make any findings. The *Jones* case is undoubtedly significant, but should we really be surprised by the decision? Surely the various committees responsible for disciplining players do not consider themselves to be immune from the scrutiny of the courts even if they adopt practices which, at best, run the risk that all the available evidence will not be heard, or, at worst, openly flout the rules of natural justice. If they do, then they are labouring under a clear misapprehension.

Furthermore, it is one thing to ban a Sunday league player and consign him to washing the car instead for his sins, but another to deprive a professional player of the right to ply his trade and earn a living. For the avoidance of doubt, it is not suggested that a Sunday league player is entitled to any less fair hearing than a professional.

The simple answer to the perceived problem of increasing judicial interference in sport is for the various governing bodies to ensure that they have in place disciplinary procedures which respect both the Rule of Law and the rules of natural justice. Adherence to those fundamental principles does not mean that informality or speed need necessarily be sacrificed, as the experience of the Atlanta Olympics showed. If the administrators of sport introduced such a process, they may find that the courts would be only too willing to adopt an approach of non-intervention. In the meantime, it is no answer to say that the law has no business poking its nose into the affairs of sport, if sport is incapable of properly conducting its affairs. Moreover, whether or not the administrators approve, the courts will continue to exercise considerable influence over many aspects of sport, most notably allegations of criminal conduct (of whatever nature) and claims for damages. In a similar vein, sport will always have to operate within the confines of the ever burdensome legislative framework imposed by central government. Accordingly, whilst the various arbitration procedures either in place, or proposed, may reduce the unedifying sight of high-profile cases passing through the courts, it would be naive to think that they will stop the procession altogether.

Chapter 2

Status of Clubs and Other Sporting Bodies

Introduction

When a sporting club or body is established, consideration must be given to its status and structure. As will be shown, the decision whether to incorporate or opt for some other status can have far-reaching implications, both in terms of the potential liability of the individual members of the club and in respect of tax and VAT. Factors to be taken into account will include the nature of the organisation, its size, purposes, source of funds and assets. The vast majority of professional clubs are incorporated, an ever-increasing number enjoying the status of public liability companies. As part of the highly developed structure of such businesses, players are employed by the clubs who will therefore be liable for torts committed by the players in the course of their employment, the legal principle which led to the involvement of Liverpool FC as second defendant in the claim brought by the Chelsea footballer, Paul Elliot (discussed in Chapter 5). At the grass roots level, most clubs will be unincorporated associations in which the club has no existence independently of its members. Accordingly, there is no question of vicarious liability arising. A negligent tackle would therefore not give rise to liability on the part of any of the other members of an unincorporated football club, unless it could be shown that they encouraged the player responsible. On the other hand, the members of a cricket club who permit the continued use of its ground when they know that balls are being hit out of the ground so as to create a reasonably foreseeable risk of injury, might incur collective responsibility in the event that someone is injured. This chapter highlights the benefits and pitfalls of running a club through the vehicle of a limited company or an unincorporated incorporation. There is also a discussion of the advantages which attach to charitable status.

Limited company or unincorporated association?

The principle of separate corporate personality, established in *Salomon v A Salomon & Co Ltd* [1897] AC 22, is the cornerstone of company law. There are a number of advantages of incorporated status. First and foremost, a limited company is a separate legal entity which exists independently of its members. It therefore survives any change in its membership, or the death, insanity or bankruptcy of all, or any, of the members. A large public company can raise substantial funds for investment purposes by a stock market flotation and, if necessary, by a subsequent rights issue.

The meteoric rise in the capital market value of Manchester United plc (from just over £47 million in June 1991 to £410 million in March 1997) has coincided with a period of unprecedented success on the field of play which has enabled the company to diversify and broaden the base of its business for the indisputable benefit of its members. In a recent report, the international accountants, Coopers & Lybrand, concluded that the football market was "overhyped and overvalued by up to £1 billion". An early exit from domestic or European cup competition may cause such shares to be more volatile than others but, historically, like the stock market itself, the long-term trend for football shares has been upwards. There are two distinct classes of investors in companies like Manchester United: first, the traditional investor who sees the shares strictly as a business proposition; and, secondly, the supporter who simply wants a slice of the club for sentimental reasons and whose framed share certificate may take pride of place in his living room. It is difficult to think of any other area of commercial activity capable of exciting such devotion, and, to that extent, shares in publicly quoted football clubs are probably unique. Both types of investor are encouraged to invest in such companies because of the twin benefits of corporate personality and the ease with which shares in public companies can be bought and sold. In those two respects, Manchester United's shares are no different to ICI, or any other publicly quoted company.

The main benefit to a small business or other organisation of setting up a company is the separation of the assets and liabilities of the company from those of its members. The articles of association of small companies invariably impose restrictions on the transfer of shares which prevents outside interference, but which still enables the entire shareholding to be sold if a take-over is desired by all concerned. The principle of the separate corporate entity means that it is the company which incurs liabilities and then calls on its shareholders according to their obligations to pay in the event of a liquidation. In the case of a company with limited liability, that would only happen if a share was partly paid. On the other hand, if money needs to be borrowed, a lender may require personal guarantees from the directors, thus exposing them to personal liability should the company fail to meet its debts. In those instances, the benefit of separate corporate personality can often seem more apparent than real. For small clubs who are able to make ends meet through subscriptions and other money-raising activities, the main disadvantage of incorporation may be the requirement to prepare and file annual returns with all the attendant expense. In very small enterprises, there may also be problems in drafting a constitution that does not exclude the minority shareholders from the management of the company, which could lead to later difficulties if relations between individual members break down.

It is a common misconception that directors can do whatever they like in the name of a company and not incur any personal liability, even when the company is their effective alter ego. That is not the case. The courts can and will lift the corporate veil in certain circumstances to find a director personally liable for a debt owed to, or a wrong committed by, his company. In *C Evans Ltd* v *Spritebrand Ltd* [1985] 1 WLR 317 the Court of Appeal concluded that a director is not automatically liable for torts committed by his company even if the company is small and the director exercises total control over it. In each case, the part which the director himself played in the commission of the tort must be examined. However, it will not always be necessary to show that a director has acted recklessly, or that he knew the company's acts to be tortious. For instance, the managing director of a company might incur personal liability if he were to instal defective temporary seating at a sporting event which collapsed under the weight of spectators.

Other forms of incorporation

The discussion so far has been devoted to companies limited by shares. A company limited by guarantee, which can be either private or public, is one where the liability of its members is limited to the amount they each undertake to contribute towards the assets of the company in the event of its being wound up. There is no obligation on the part of the members to make any contribution whilst the company remains a going concern. This type of arrangement is popular with professional and other representative bodies since it usually receives its funding from subscriptions and benevolent sources. The British Olympic Association is a prime example. A company may also be unlimited, in which case there is no restriction on the liability of its members to contribute to its assets. Not surprisingly, there are comparatively few such companies in existence, despite the more relaxed rules on the production of accounts which apply to them. To complete the picture, a company may be incorporated by royal charter. The power to confer that privilege arises out of the common law royal prerogative, as opposed to any legislative provision, company or otherwise.

Unincorporated clubs

An unincorporated club or other association has no legal personality recognised by the law (except for taxation purposes, which are discussed in Chapter 3). Instead, a personal relationship exists between each of the members of the club, giving rise to collective responsibility for liabilities incurred in the name of the club. Accordingly, when an officer of such a club undertakes a particular task on its behalf, he owes a duty of care to his fellow members and will be liable to them if he is in breach of it (see *Jones* v *Northampton Borough Council* (1990) *The Times*, 21 May). That liability arises out of the contractual relationship created as between each of the members of the association as they join.

Since an unincorporated club is itself a fiction, it should sue and be sued in the name of one or more of its members. Difficulties may be experienced in suing for a breach of contract or other wrong (*e.g.* a failure on the part of a supplier to supply goods or services which have been paid for). However, a contract which, on its face, purports to have been entered into by, or with, an unincorporated club is not necessarily void. The member(s) who made the contract, such as the secretary or committee, may be held to have contracted personally and be personally liable on the contract (see *Bradley Egg Farm Limited* v *Clifford* [1943] 2 All ER 378). Contractual commitments should therefore be entered into in the name of one or more of the members of the club, not the name of the club itself. Furthermore, under the law of agency, the member(s) who made the agreement may be held to have contracted on behalf of the other members of the club. In those circumstances, a representative action can be brought by or against one or more of the members, including the trustees of the funds of the club, as representing the others. This course avoids the need to join numerous defendants to the proceedings. In effect, it is a minor representative action.

The common conception of representative actions is large-scale litigation against pharmaceutical and tobacco companies where the claims share common ground and seek similar relief, such as the litigation against the US tobacco giant BAT. It has only been since the early 1980s that a claim for damages in this country has been capable of being brought as a representative action (see *EMI* v *Riley* [1981] 2 All ER 838). The represented plaintiffs must have the same interest, share a common grievance and seek relief which is beneficial to the other parties who are interested in the outcome of the litigation. A damages claim can also now be brought against representative defendants. In that event, *all* the members of the club would be prima facie liable (*i.e.* not just those who are sued). Each individual member would then have to argue why he should be excused from liability. It is therefore crucial to ensure that unincorporated associations have adequate insurance cover to avoid the eventuality which befell the committee members of Blackburn Rovers Football Club when it was confronted with a claim following the collapse of a grandstand (see *Brown* v *Lewis* (1896) 12 TLR 455). In the absence of such protection, those unfortunate enough to be sued will have no option other than to serve contribution notices against their fellow defendants and consider third-party proceedings claiming an indemnity against any other members who are worth pursuing.

Achieving charitable status

The majority of sports clubs do not enjoy the considerable fiscal advantages which charitable status confers, as Chapter 3 will show. It appears to be settled law that a gift for the promotion of a given sport is not, without more, charitable. For example, in *Re Nottage* [1895] 2 Ch 649 the testator established a trust to provide a cup for the most successful yacht of the season, stating that his objective was to encourage the sport of yacht racing. It was held by the Court of Appeal that the gift was one for the encouragement of a mere sport which, although it might benefit the public, was not charitable. A similar conclusion was arrived at in *Re Clifford* (1911) 106 LT 14 (angling); *Re Patten* [1929] 2 Ch 276 (cricket); *IRC* v *Baddeley* [1955] AC 572 (moral, social and physical training and recreation); *IRC* v *City of Glasgow Police Athletic Association* [1953] AC 380 (all forms of athletic sports and general pastimes); and *Re King* [1931] WN 232 (sport in general).

However, trusts for sporting purposes will be effective if they are drafted so as to bring them within the scope of the Recreational Charities Act 1958. Section 1(1) of the Act provides that it shall be, and shall be deemed always to have been, charitable, to provide, or assist in providing facilities for recreation or other leisure-time occupations if the facilities are provided in the interest of social welfare. This is subject to the *caveat* that the trust will not be charitable unless it is for the public benefit. Additionally, section 1(2) goes on to provide that the requirement that facilities must be provided in the interest of social welfare is not satisfied unless:

(1) it is provided with the object of improving the conditions of life for the persons for whom the facilities are primarily intended; and

(2) either (a) those persons have need of such facilities by reason of their youth, age, infirmity or disablement, poverty or social and economic circumstances, or (b) the facilities are to be available to the members or female members of the public at large.

To that end, the trust instrument must be construed in order to determine whether a particular charitable purpose is advanced by the sporting activity which it is intended should benefit. Where the promotion of sport is ancillary to a charitable object, it will itself be charitable. *IRC v McMullen* [1981] AC 1 concerned the legal effect of the Football Association Youth Trust whose object was to organise or assist in the organisation and provision of facilities which would enable and encourage students at schools and universities to play football or other games and sports, and thereby assist in ensuring that due attention was given to the physical education and development of such pupils, as well as the occupation of their minds. With a view to furthering that object, the deed encouraged the provision of such facilities as playing-fields, equipment etc. The House of Lords held that the purpose of the deed was not merely to promote the playing of football in schools and universities, but also to promote the physical education and development of students in addition to their formal education. Accordingly, the deed created a valid charitable trust for the advancement of education, since sporting activities contributed towards a balanced education. By contrast, the promotion of specific games, as distinct from recreation, without any necessary correlation with education, is not charitable (see *IRC v Trustees of the Football Association Youth Trust* [1977] TR 189).

In *Guild* v *IRC* [1992] 2 All ER 10 the House of Lords considered section 1(1) of the 1958 Act in the context of a bequest "to be used in connection with a sports centre in North Berwick" and also "some similar purpose in connection with sport". The "social welfare" requirement was found to have been satisfied. It seems, therefore, that social welfare connotes some element of provision for others, and an organisation acting solely for its own benefit would fail to qualify (as well as falling foul of the public benefit requirement). The judgments in *McMullen* and *Guild* both affirmed the pre-1958 Act decision in *Re Marriette* [1915] 2 Ch 384 where the testator made the following bequest:

> "£1,000 to the Governing Body of Aldenham School for the purpose of building Eton fives courts or squash racket courts, or for some similar purpose that shall be decided by a majority of the housemasters at the time of my death,"

together with a further £100 to the headmaster:

> "upon trust to use the interest to provide a prize for some event in the school athletic sports."

Eve J held that both limbs of the bequest qualified as valid charitable legacies, and ruled that a student's bodily and physical development was no less important than learning Latin or Greek. He must have had a premonition when he also observed that to leave boys at large and to their own devices during their leisure hours would probably result in them quickly relapsing into something approaching barbarism! In a similar vein, a gift for the promotion of athletic, social and cultural activities of a students' union was held to be charitable as furthering the educational purposes of a college (see *London Hospital Medical College* v *IRC* [1976] 2 All ER 113).

A gift for the promotion of a sport in an army regiment was held to be charitable since it increased the army's efficiency (see *Re Gray* [1925] Ch 362). In *IRC* v *City of Glasgow Police Athletic Association* (above) doubts were expressed about the decision in *Re Gray*, but there can be no dispute that an army is more efficient if its soldiers are physically fit, which has a corresponding benefit to the public.

In conclusion, charitable status may be available to a sporting body (or gift) if it provides leisure or recreation facilities which are for the benefit of the public. The same objective may be achieved where facilities, financial or otherwise, are provided to assist the development and physical education of young people. The definition of "education" has broadened considerably even since the enlightened analysis of Eve J in *Re Mariette*, and the judgments in *McMullen* suggest that it is now capable of including activities which do not have as their strict objective an increase in knowledge. Historically, clubs have not been successful in applying to register as charities, although the Charity Commissioners appear to be sympathetic towards a relaxation of the qualification criteria However, any material change is likely to require the intervention of Parliament. In the meantime, the larger sporting bodies which are attracted to the possibility of establishing a sporting foundation can find guidance in a leaflet entitled *Sport and Charitable Status* which is published jointly by the Sports Council, the Central Council of Physical Recreation and the National Playing Fields Association (see Appendix for addresses of those bodies).

Chapter 3

Taxation of Sport

Introduction

Since the Second World War, successive governments have imposed an increasingly heavy financial burden on sport through tax and other fiscal legislation. That burden is reflected, principally, in the amount which sport contributes annually to the Treasury in tax, and to HM Customs and Excise in VAT payments. A cameo example was the 1996 European Football Championships, which generated approximately £65 million in taxes for the Treasury, yet the financial assistance provided by central government for the staging of the tournament was small by comparison. The other pressure which the tax requirements impose is felt by those responsible for administering the 150,000 or so sports organisations in the country. Despite assurances to the contrary made by the Inland Revenue, the new self-assessment regime is likely to compound the administrative burden on club secretaries and committees. It is not surprising, therefore, that many argue for a reduction in the tax burden inflicted on sport. However, at the professional level, sport is now firmly established as part of the entertainment industry, and it seems unlikely that the Treasury will create special tax exemptions for sport (although it has been compelled to do so in order to comply with EC VAT directives, as will be shown). In this chapter, general guidance will be given on the way in which tax affects sport, together with an introduction to the role of VAT. A more detailed examination of the issues raised can be found in publications such as *Tax and Financial Planning for Sportsmen and Entertainers*, 2nd ed (Butterworths). One of the co-authors of that book, Richard Baldwin, has also written several helpful articles in the *British Association for Sport and the Law Journal*. The complexity of tax law underlines the fact that this particular corner of the playing-field, perhaps more than any other, will almost inevitably call for specialist accountancy and tax advice.

Taxation of clubs

General principles

The income and capital gains of a sports club or similar body may be liable to corporation tax even if it does not have the status of a limited company. The fact that no special tax concessions exist is often overlooked by those who run sports clubs, with potentially serious consequences. It has already been noted that at grass roots level clubs are typically unincorporated associations and, therefore, come within the definition of "company" for corporation tax purposes. The Income and Corporation Taxes Act 1988 and the Taxation of Chargeable Gains Act 1992 render a "company" (which definition includes unincorporated associations) liable for corporation tax on any income or chargeable gains it may receive. Recent cases have confirmed that although an unincorporated association has no separate identity, it is the association and not the individual members who are liable to tax (see *Worthing Rugby Football Club Trustees* v *IRC* [1985] 1 WLR 409; and *Frampton* v *IRC* [1987] STC 273).

Accordingly, a club will be prima facie liable to pay corporation tax on income derived from trading or similar activities, rents received, and interest on monies invested in banks, building societies etc. If a club incurs expenses in the course of generating an income from trading activities, those expenses are generally allowed against the trading profits for the same accounting period. A trading loss also qualifies for corporation tax relief, provided the club would have been liable for tax had it made a profit. The disposal of an asset at a profit will be assessable to capital gains tax (although the costs of acquiring and disposing of the asset are generally taken into account in calculating the amount of the gain). If a club considers that it may be liable to corporation tax or capital gains tax, it should give details immediately to its local tax office. The financial penalties for non-compliance can be harsh – the Inland Revenue may seek to recover tax for the previous six years of a fund raising activity which has not been declared – and the officers of clubs can also render themselves personally liable in certain circumstances.

Members' subscriptions

As a general rule, subscriptions and other contributions made by individual club members to the club's funds are not regarded as part of the club's taxable income. Similarly, the day-to-day expense of running the club are not normally deductible against tax. Therefore, any shortfall or surplus resulting from those items is not usually taken into account when assessing the club's corporation tax position. Non-taxable contributions include payments made by members for goods or facilities provided to them by the club.

However, charges made to members for their private use of club facilities are not included, such as the hire of a sports hall or clubhouse for a party or a wedding. For over 90 years private sports clubs which have made profits from funding provided by sources other than members' subscriptions have been taxed on those profits (see *Carlisle and Silloth Golf Club* v *Smith* [1913] 3 KB 75 which concerned income derived from green fees).

Fund-raising

Fund-raising activities such as fetes, jumble sales, firework displays and dinner dances are regarded as trading activities by the Inland Revenue, and any profits derived from them are liable to corporation tax. The exception to this rule requires a number of conditions to be satisfied, namely:

(1) where the organisation does not regularly trade; *and*
(2) the activity in question is not in competition with other traders; *and*
(3) the profits are given to charities, or are otherwise used for charitable purposes; *and*
(4) the public support the activity mainly because they know that any profits will be going to charity.

Any profit derived from prize draws, raffles and lotteries is generally liable to tax, and care needs to be taken to ensure that the requirements of the Lotteries and Amusements Act 1976 are adhered to. If the activity is organised and run independently of the club in question (*e.g.* by a committee of trustees), any profit generated may then be donated to the club on a tax-free basis, subject to Inland Revenue approval. If a club obtains funding in the form of advertising or sponsorship, whether in cash or in kind, the Inland Revenue will seek to recover corporation tax on that source of income.

National Lottery grants

The approach currently adopted by the Inland Revenue is that capital grants made by the Sports Lottery Fund towards sports projects engaged in taxable activities will reduce the tax relief available to clubs on the capital expenditure incurred by them. In other words, for example, if a bowls club builds a new clubhouse with lottery monies, any tax relief which would otherwise be available on the cost of construction will be reduced. Other grants may be either capital or revenue, and the treatment of each differs for tax purposes. A discussion of that distinction is beyond the scope of this book.

Capital expenditure

Significant capital expenditure on development projects raises important considerations regarding the status of the investment for both tax and VAT purposes. In 1969, Burnley Football Club demolished a stand which was no longer safe, and replaced it with a new stand at a cost of over £200,000. The club subsequently advanced two grounds in support of the contention that it was entitled to set off the financial investment in the new stand against its profits for the purposes of corporation tax, namely:

(1) that it was a "repair of premises" pursuant to section 130 of the Income and Corporation Taxes Act 1970; or

(2) that it represented capital expenditure on the provision of plant for the purposes of the Club's business under section 41 of the Finance Act 1971.

The Presiding Special Tax Commissioner upheld the first ground, but rejected the second. He found that the playing area and the spectator stands were part of an inseparable whole, in a physical, functional and commercial sense. Central to his decision was a finding that the spectators paid money to occupy the stands and watch football matches, and participated in the games by lending their support to them. The Inspector of Taxes appealed, and Vinleott J reversed the Commissioner's decision, holding that no part of the ground, except the pitch itself, was necessary to the performance of the Club's central activity of arranging football matches (see *Brown (Inspector of Taxes)* v *Burnley Football and Athletic Co Ltd* [1980] 3 All ER 244).

Since the *Burnley* case, certain expenditure on buildings to which safety certificates apply under the sports ground safety legislation (see Chapter 8) has been allowed for capital allowance purposes by successive Finance Acts. In his final report on the Hillsborough Tragedy, Lord Justice Taylor remarked on the tax anomaly which allowed football clubs to set off payments for players as allowable revenue expenditure, but not ground improvements. He concluded that the encouragement of expenditure on ground improvements by tax concession was ripe for re-examination. In the light of that recommendation, the relevant statutory provisions were consolidated into the Capital Allowance Act 1990 (see ss 55, 69 and 70) and if the facts of the *Burnley* case were to be repeated, a different outcome might result.

Charities

The difficulties associated with achieving charitable status have already been discussed, but the struggle is often worthwhile as special tax rules apply if a sports club, or other body, is a charity. The principal tax advantages which charitable status attracts are as follows:

- no tax is payable on investment income, rental income, or capital gains, which are applied for charitable purposes;
- inheritance tax and capital gains tax are not payable on gifts made to a charity;
- tax relief is available to a charity on deeds of covenant made in its favour;
- tax relief is available to individuals and corporations on deeds of covenant made in favour of charities;
- premises which are occupied wholly, or in part, by a charity for charitable purposes are entitled to a mandatory 80% relief against the business rates payable, with a discretionary power to grant relief of up to 100%.

Advice on the tax position of charities can be obtained from the Inland Revenue Claims Branch, Charity Division, Magdalen House, Trinity Road, Bootle, Merseyside L69 9BB.

Taxation of individuals

General principles

Individual sportsmen and women obtain funding from a variety of sources. In addition to a salary, players often receive prize money and payments from sponsors and advertisers. Professional footballers, cricketers and, now, rugby players, are employed by their clubs, and any payments made pursuant to the employment relationship are subject to tax (under Schedule E). Under Premier League and Football League rules, earnings cannot be paid to a service company in order to reduce the tax liability of a player since it is the player who is contracted to his club, not the company. Other benefits, such as payments for international matches, win-bonuses and players' pools, also form part of a player's earnings for tax purposes.

Signing-on fees

A signing-on fee paid to a player when he transfers from one club to another will prima facie be assessable to income tax. In order for such a payment to qualify for tax exemption, the player will have to show that he has given up a valuable right. In the past, difficulties have arisen over payments made to players for relinquishing their amateur status and turning professional. For instance, in *Jarrold* v *Boustead* [1964] 41 TC 701 an amateur footballer who received such a payment did not have to pay tax on it. However, where an amateur player received an additional payment which tied him to the purchasing club for the rest of his career, that element of the signing-on fee was held to be liable to tax (see *Riley* v *Colgan* [1967] 44 TC 481). Since 1987, tax relief has been available to amateurs who turn professional, and cases which have been decided since then suggest that the loss of amateur status is minimal.

Golden handshakes

The majority of payments that transferring clubs make to players when they move to a new club will be taxable as ordinary earnings. Accordingly, when the England goalkeeper, Peter Shilton, transferred from Nottingham Forest to Southampton, the £75,000 payment Shilton received from Forest was held to have been an emolument from his employment under section 181(1) of the Income and Corporation Taxes Act 1970, and liable to tax. The House of Lords rejected the player's argument that the payment was a golden handshake from Forest in order to encourage his transfer and thus reduce that club's wage bill. The payment was held to be an element of the transfer contract and part of his continuing employment with Southampton (see *Shilton* v *Wilmhurst* [1991] STC 88). It should also be noted that a player who receives a proportion of his transfer fee will have to declare it for tax purposes. Such payments are not within the scope of the "golden handshake" legislation which exempts certain one-off payments from tax. However, a player's share of a transfer fee is often spread over the duration of his contract and the tax burden can similarly be spread.

Testimonial payments

By contrast, extraordinary payments which have been made to players to mark an illustrious career, or which were unique to the players concerned, have been held by the courts to be non-taxable. A testimonial match or season is a benefit many players enjoy towards the end of a sporting career, and can often generate a substantial cash windfall. For those who have no other immediate source of income, testimonials are essential, and the status of such payments for tax purposes is therefore of crucial importance. In 1920 a benefit match was held for the Kent cricketer, James Seymour, by his county. The House of Lords held that the proceeds of the match were a gift or donation from an appreciative public and were not income assessable to income tax (see *Seymour* v *Reed* [1927] AC 554). However, where a payment automatically accrued to a footballer after playing for a specified number of years, the benefit was held to be assessable to tax since it did not have the hallmark of a payment to a particular individual (see *Davis* v *Harrison* [1927] 11 TC 707). Similarly, a cricketer was assessed on payments he received from spectators which were permitted by Lancashire League rules for players scoring more than 50 runs (see *Moorhouse* v *Dooland* [1954] 36 TC 701).

Benefit matches

In a similar vein, following their success in the 1966 World Cup final, the England players were paid a £1,000 win bonus by the FA, in addition to their basic match fee. The payments were held to have had the quality of a testimonial or accolade rather than remuneration for services rendered (see *Moore* v *Griffiths* [1978] 3 All ER 309). The Inland Revenue no longer contends that such benefits are taxable. However, to avoid any problems there should be no contractual right to a benefit match in the player's contract. Additionally, the Inland Revenue may still take an interest if a benefit match coincides with the termination of a player's contract (*e.g.* when he is transferred to another club, or retires from the game). The organisation of benefit matches are best placed in the hands of independent trustees, rather than the player's club, thereby avoiding any suggestion that the proceeds of the match derive from a contractual arrangement. When the match itself takes place, only a small admission charge should be levied, leaving the player to rely on the generosity of spectators by way of voluntary donations. The mainly gratuitous nature of the funds generated in that way again serves to scotch any suggestion that such funds qualify as usual remuneration.

Value Added Tax

General principles

Value added tax was introduced by the Finance Act of 1972 and, since then, its scope and application have become increasingly influenced by a desire on the part of EC Member States to harmonise their respective internal VAT arrangements. The current regime is governed by the VAT Act 1994, which should be read in conjunction with the Finance Act 1997. Although they are by no means exhaustive, the following points are worthy of mention in the sporting context.

- The basic principle is that VAT is levied whenever goods or services are *supplied* in the United Kingdom.
- The transfer of a player between UK-resident clubs represents a supply of services, and the transfer fee is subject to VAT. When Alan Shearer was transferred from Blackburn to Newcastle in the summer of 1996, the VAT charge on the transfer fee of £15 million exceeded £2.25 million.
- If a UK club buys a player from an EC club, the *supply* is deemed to take place in the country where the customer (the UK club) has its permanent place of business. Accordingly, when Dennis Bergkamp was transferred from Inter Milan to Arsenal in 1995, the English club was liable for the VAT due on the transfer fee, although it was entitled to use the reverse charge procedure under section 8 of the VAT Act 1994 to clawback its liability (*i.e.* the input/output tax set-off).
- If sporting services, such as a professional footballer, are supplied from the United Kingdom to another EC club, the price received by the seller will be exempt from VAT as long as the supply is received by the EC club for the purpose of its business (which a player would be). Transfers of players to and from clubs which are not based in the European Community are zero-rated for VAT purposes.
- VAT is not normally charged on any payment made to a player in the form of a signing-on fee, or by way of levy paid to the sport's governing body.

- Where a club or individual provides publicity for a sponsor and receives sponsorship income in return, VAT should be charged to the sponsor if the provider of the service is VAT registered.
- Admission charges are liable to VAT. Some clubs attempt to reduce their VAT liability by allowing admission to an event by the purchase of a programme (programmes, being booklets, are zero-rated). However, the reading content of the programme must be substantial to avoid the charge that it is simply a glorified ticket, and Customs and Excise will still insist on an element of the purchase price being attributed to admission.
- The sale of advertisements in programmes is subject to VAT. Advertising which appears on hoardings in or around a ground or stadium qualifies as a licence to use land and is therefore exempt from VAT, although that may simply shift the VAT burden on to the owner or tenant of the premises in question.
- Entry fees to sporting or other competitions involving physical recreation where the entire entry fee is returned in the form of prizes, or where the competition is organised by a non-profit-making body established for sporting purposes, are exempt from VAT.

HM Customs and Excise ruled out of bounds

From 1 January 1990 Customs and Excise began charging VAT on the sporting activities of non-profit-making organisations, in contravention of EC law. Considerable pressure to reverse that policy was brought to bear on the Chancellor of the Exchequer by a number of recreational and sporting bodies, including the Central Council for Physical Recreation (CCPR) and the Foundation for Sport and the Arts. In July 1993 the Government finally acknowledged that VAT which had been charged across a broad range of sporting and recreational services would have to be repaid (see VAT Notice 701/45/94 *Sport and Physical Education*). The Value Added Tax (Sport, Physical Education and Fund-Raising Events) Order 1994 (SI 1994/687) came into force on 1 April 1994. The Order extended Group 10 of Schedule 6 to the VAT Act 1983 (since replaced by the 1994 Act) to provide exemption from VAT for certain services supplied by non-profit-making bodies to people taking part in sport or physical education, and, belatedly, implemented Article 13 of the Sixth Council Directive (77/388) on the Harmonisation of the Laws of EC Member States relating to turnover taxes.

No less than 113 non-profit-making sporting activities qualify for exemption and the repayment figure was put at £150 million in some quarters of the press. Whatever the actual size of the bill to the Government may have been, the fact that the money had to be repaid gave rise to a further debate, namely the entitlement (or otherwise) of the individual members of golf clubs to recover the VAT which they had originally been charged as part of their annual subscriptions, or whether the clubs were entitled to retain the refunds to be distributed for the benefit of their members generally. At the request of the CCPR, Andrew Park QC, a leading tax counsel, provided an opinion in which he concluded that there was no legal obligation on clubs to make refunds. Golf clubs were in the vanguard of the movement which eventually led to the Government climbdown, but whether exemption from VAT will prove to be a benefit to golf clubs remains to be seen. Playing members will no longer have to pay VAT on their subscriptions, although the fact that green fees and social membership subscriptions remain taxable means that clubs will still have to register for VAT. Additionally, the club itself will not be able to reclaim VAT charged on purchases required for course maintenance. As a general observation, the non-sporting activities run by sports clubs, such as bars and restaurants, will remain subject to VAT and, if the turnover from that source exceeds the VAT registration threshold, a club would still have to register, if only for that reason. Finally, it should be noted that only services supplied by non-profit-making sports organisations are exempt from VAT, not those provided by commercial organisations run for profit.

Chapter 4

The Field of Play – Part I

Crime on the field of play

Introduction

To attempt to separate the issues discussed in this chapter and those in Chapter 5 is a little artificial since the two share a certain amount of common ground. Nevertheless, it may help to crystallise in the reader's mind the particular considerations applicable to the criminal and civil law. A good starting-point is the proposition that a deliberate and/or reckless tackle which causes injury gives rise to a prima facie criminal offence, and is also a tort. That is especially so where the tackle is in breach of the laws of the particular game, as it invariably will be (see *R v Venna* [1975] 3 All ER 788, where the judgment of Bramwell LJ in *R v Bradshaw* (1878) 14 Cox CC was cited with approval).

From the outset, it should be noted that the Latin maxim *volenti non fit injuria* has no application in the context of deliberate or reckless breaches of the laws of any game. In other words, it is no defence for a defendant to say that a fellow competitor expressly or impliedly consented to a battery, whether intentional or reckless. Someone who strikes a blow which is out of all proportion to the occasion will be found liable unless he can prove that it was an accident, or that he acted out of self-defence (see the judgment of Lord Denning in *Lane v Holloway* [1968] 1 QB 379 at 386). Liability will arise irrespective of whether a defendant fails to exercise the degree of care which is appropriate in the circumstances, or if he acts in a way which the plaintiff cannot be expected to have consented to.

However, whilst a deliberate shoulder charge, for example, would undoubtedly constitute a battery if it was inflicted on an unwilling passenger in an attempt to gain entry to a crowded train, such a blow, provided it was not disproportionately violent, would not be unlawful if committed on a soccer pitch because the "victim" is deemed to have consented to an act which the laws of the game reasonably permit. Whether or not something is reasonable is, of course, a question of fact and degree. It is conceivable, therefore, that an act could be permitted by the rules of a particular game, but be ruled unreasonable as a matter of law. What is, or is not, in the public interest gives the courts broad scope to decide whether a particular act is criminal.

This discussion inevitably begs the question: how is it possible to reconcile the objectives involved in boxing with the limitations which the law imposes? When a boxer delivers a fierce upper-cut with the intention of knocking his opponent out, there can be little doubt that he intends to cause injury. Yet the lawfulness of such a blow is not questioned. It is an example of the socially accepted theory (which is not shared by everyone) that the assumed value of the sport is deemed to justify the victim's consent to the other's attempt to knock him out.

Conversely, where two teenage youths decided to settle an argument with a fist fight and one sustained a bloody nose and bruises, the other was found guilty of assault occasioning actual body harm (see *Attorney-General's Reference (No 6 of 1980)* [1981] 2 All ER 1057). The judgment was based firmly on the principle that it was not in the public interest to allow people to cause each other physical harm for no good reason. The same principle applies to so-called "prize fights" which the courts have regularly found to be batteries (see *R v Coney* (1882) 8 QBD 534). Any entertainment value of such contests is deemed to be outweighed by the lack of any regulation, or protection, with the attendant risk of severe physical injury. The position, therefore, is that most fights will be unlawful irrespective of the consent of the participants, with properly conducted games and sports being the notable exception.

The limitations of consent

The feature of certain sports which sets them apart from other social activities is the element of physical contact. However, the law protects competitors by imposing a limit on their right to consent to the infliction of physical harm on themselves. At the most extreme level, consent to being killed is ineffective. Where the act has some social utility recognised by the law as valid, it is a question of balancing the degree of harm which will or may be caused against the value of the intended purpose. The law therefore imposes limits on the level of physical contact to which a person is capable of consenting. In *R v Venna* (above) the Court of Appeal endorsed the principle established by Bramwell LJ in *R* v *Bradshaw* (1878) (above), that deliberate, intentional and/or reckless violent foulplay gives rise to criminal liability. In *R* v *Billinghurst* [1977] Crim LR 553 the defendant was the first rugby union player to be prosecuted and then convicted of inflicting grievous bodily harm on an opponent during a game. There was no dispute that what the defendant did was not done in the course of the playing the game.

The House of Lords ruled on the effectiveness of adults consenting to sado-masochistic acts in *R* v *Brown* [1994] AC 21. In the course of his judgment, Lord Mustill made the following observations on the consensual element involved in certain sports (at pp 265-266):

> "Some sports, such as the various codes of football, have deliberate bodily contact as an essential element. They lie at the mid-point between fighting, where the participant knows that his opponent will try to harm him, and the milder sports where there is at most an acknowledgment that someone may be accidentally hurt."

His Lordship continued:

> "In the contact sports each player knows and by taking part agrees that an opponent may from time to time inflict upon his body (for example by a rugby tackle) what would otherwise be a painful battery. By taking part he also assumes the risk that the deliberate contact may have unintended effects, conceivably of sufficient severity to amount to grievous bodily harm. But he does not agree that this more serious kind of injury may be inflicted deliberately."

Lord Mustill conceded that that simple analysis concealed a number of difficulties, the main one being to identify the point at which an implied consent to some degree of harm becomes too much for the law to tolerate (see "Problems of proving intention" below).

The Law Commission's recommendations

In February 1994 the Law Commission published a consultation paper *Consent and Offences against the Person* (Law Com No 134). Comments were invited on whether or not outlawing consent to, amongst other practices, sporting violence required legislation. Following representations, the Commission produced a further consultation paper in December 1995 (Law Com No 139). In the revised proposals, criminal liability for the reckless causation of "seriously disabling injury" will not arise unless three conditions are satisfied, namely:

(1) that the player in question was aware of a risk of a seriously disabling injury;

(2) that the risk was not a reasonable risk for him to take, having regard to all the circumstances known to him (including the consent of the other participants to the risk inherent in playing according to the rules of the sport in question); and

(3) the injury resulted in permanent bodily injury, permanent disfigurement etc (*i.e.* "seriously disabling injury" – as defined).

The Commission provisionally recommends that if the conditions are not satisfied, it should be a matter for the sporting bodies themselves to discipline, and not for the criminal courts to intervene. It cites the example of a fast bowler who would only be at risk of criminal prosecution under the proposals if his conduct is clearly outside the rules of the game. If he ignores warnings from the umpire and persists in bowling dangerously with the result that a batsman is injured, he is liable to be convicted of a criminal offence if the court was sure that he intended to inflict injury. Even if that intention could not be proved, he would still be convicted if he inflicted serious injury on the batsman and a court concluded that he was aware of the risk that he might inflict such injury and the risk was not a reasonable one for him to take.

A scheme of recognition for lawful sports

Another allied issue addressed by the Law Commission in its consultation paper No 139 is the establishment of a scheme of recognition for those sports and martial arts activities where there is a risk of physical injury (see Part XIII). In particular, concern was expressed at the lack of any proper internal regulations or controls with certain martial arts "sports". By contrast, boxing, the rules of which permit the intentional infliction of injury, has a highly developed system for containing the risk of injury. The body which, it is envisaged, would be responsible for deciding whether or not a sport should be recognised as lawful is the Sports Council. The Commission recommends that if the rules of a recognised lawful sport permit the intentional infliction of injury, the criminal law should sanction those rules, and the recognition body would then be responsible for ensuring that the risks involved are properly controlled.

Participation in an unrecognised sport would be prima facie unlawful and subject to the scrutiny of the criminal law. A criminal court faced with an allegation that a seriously disabling injury was caused by reckless conduct on a sports field could determine more easily whether the risk of causing such injury was a reasonable one for the defendant to take if the court had available the rules of the sport as approved by the recognition body.

Compulsory games

A lacuna may exist in cases involving compulsory games in schools where both the plaintiff and defendant are likely to be non-voluntary participants. It is suggested that such a defendant should not be deprived of the protection which might otherwise be available to him. In other words, an unintentional infliction of physical injury ought not to constitute a battery by virtue of the fact that the "victim" is playing in the game out of compulsion rather than choice.

Problems of proving intention

The acceptance of the risk of injury and the problems associated with proving intention are, to a large extent, interlinked. In an obvious case, there will be relatively little difficulty proving that a blow struck by one participant against another was intentional, or at least reckless. When play stops in an ice-hockey match and opposing players engage in a brawl (an occurrence which seems to happen with remarkable frequency) those involved will prima facie commit an offence of criminal assault and also contravene the Public Order Act 1986 in one or more respects. Similarly, when the final whistle blows, issues of consent and *volenti* fall away to expose any conduct which transgresses the criminal law. In *R v Kamara* (1988) *The Times*, 15 April a footballer pleaded guilty to a charge of causing grevious bodily harm after he broke the jaw of an opposing player in the tunnel after a game. The cases of *R v Bishop* (1986) *The Times*, 12 October and *RN v Russell* (1994) *The Times*, 23 February both involved convictions arising out of violent foul play during the course of rugby union matches. The Everton and Scotland footballer, Duncan Ferguson, was also convicted (while a Rangers player) for an assault on an opposing player during the course of a match and received a custodial sentence for what was not his first such transgression (see *R v Ferguson* (1995) *The Times*, 12 October).

However, such blatant examples of foul play are likely to be the exception rather than the rule. In many physical contact sports, the division between lawful and unlawful conduct is often blurred, no more so than in rugby union where the practice of rucking and mauling is expressly permitted by the rules of the sport. Similarly, a reasonable shoulder charge delivered in the course of a game of football is lawful according to the laws of that game and is not rendered unlawful if, by misfortune, it causes personal injury or, worse still, death. Consequently, as between participants it will often be difficult to show that physical injury has been inflicted negligently, let alone deliberately or recklessly. It may sound a trite statement, but whether an intentional foul (or, for that matter, a mistake or an error of judgment) is capable of giving rise to criminal and/or civil liability depends on all the facts and circumstances of each particular case.

Recklessness – the present position

Until such times as the Law Commission's recommendations are enshrined in statute, or the House of Lords sweeps away the existing common law, the test for recklessness in assault and battery is the one formulated in *R v Cunningham* [1957] 2 QB 396 (see also *DPP v Parmenter* [1992] 1 AC 699). Recklessness in common assault involves foresight of the possibility that the victim would apprehend the application of immediate and unlawful personal violence, and the defendant taking that risk. In battery, recklessness involves foresight of the possibility that the victim will be subjected to unlawful force, however slight, and the defendant, again, taking that risk. The *mens rea* of assault occasioning actual bodily harm is the same as for common assault, the additional dimension being the requirement to prove that the assault in fact caused actual bodily harm. "Bodily harm" includes any hurt or injury calculated to interfere with the health or comfort of the victim, and is capable of including psychiatric injury (but not mere emotions, like fear, distress or panic). It is also conceivable that an offence contrary to either section 18 (wounding with intent to do grievous bodily harm), or section 20 (inflicting grievous bodily harm), of the Offences Against the Persons Act 1861 might be committed in a sporting setting. For a discussion of the requirements pertaining to those two offences, the reader is referred to *Archbold*, para 19-202 *et seq*.

The rules of the game

The rules of the sport in question are clearly relevant in assessing the standard of care which the participants are entitled to expect from one another, but they are not decisive. A breach of a rule which is designed solely to encourage fair play does not automatically amount to negligence. In *Condon v Basi* [1985] 1 WLR 866 the plaintiff was an amateur footballer who broke his leg in a tackle during a local league match. In his judgment, Lord Donaldson cited the Australian case of *Rootes v Shelton* [1968] ALR 33 and approved of the view that whilst a tackle may break the rules of the game, that fact, by itself, is not conclusive of negligence. Although both cases involved civil claims for damages, as opposed to criminal prosecutions, if proving a breach of the rules of the particular game will not necessarily found liability in negligence, it is difficult to see why the position should be any different where a criminal act is alleged. Support for that proposition can be traced back to the late nineteenth century when Hawkins J (see *R v Moore* (1989) 14 TLR 229) made the following statement when refusing to allow the rules of football to be put in evidence by the Crown:

> "... for it is not criminal and not necessarily either dangerous or malicious to break them."

On the other hand, conduct may be dangerous (and *a fortiori* unreasonable) even though it does *not* infringe any particular rule (see *Affutu-Nartoy* v *Clarke* (1984) *The Times*, 9 February). Furthermore, in *R v Bradshaw* (above), Bramwell LJ admitted evidence of the rules of the game at the request of the defence as tending to show that the defendant was not actuated by any malicious motive or intention and was not acting in a manner which he knew was likely to cause death or injury. It is submitted that the approach adopted by Bramwell LJ is correct, since the rules of the game are clearly a factor of which the court must take account when considering the defendant's conduct.

Drawing all the various strands together, the following principles emerge:

- the limit of a player's consent is to be judged according to all the circumstances of the case, including the rules of the game and the social utility of the act in question;
- however, there can be no question of a player consenting, expressly or impliedly, to a deliberate or reckless assault;

- although an intention to inflict injury may be difficult to prove in the context of fast-moving physical contact sports, inferences to be drawn from the facts surrounding the incident may support a finding of recklessness; and
- a finding to the effect that a sporting injury was inflicted deliberately, will almost certainly lead to the conclusion that the conduct complained of was also negligent.

Practical considerations

This whole debate leads to the inevitable inquiry: if a plaintiff can establish, on a balance of probabilities, that the defendant was negligent, what difference does it make if he is not also convicted of a criminal offence? The answer is probably 'not much'. The obvious benefit is that, having regard to the differing standards of proof in criminal and civil proceedings, a successful criminal conviction may well concentrate a defendant's mind to settle a civil action based on the same allegation. It will certainly be a very high evidential hurdle for him to overcome. Whilst the criminal courts are empowered to award compensation (under s 35 of the Powers of Criminal Courts Act 1973), it is very unlikely that a victim will obtain adequate recompense from that source for any injury which he may have suffered. If he desires a more scientific assessment of his damages, he will either have to sue, or submit a claim to the Criminal Injuries Compensation Authority. Paradoxically, a finding to the effect that an injury was inflicted deliberately may be positively harmful to a plaintiff's interests since it could invalidate any insurance cover of which the assailant may have had the benefit, as well as taking him outside the scope of his employment if that is a relevant consideration.

Secondary liability

As the Law Commission has recently noted, the violent sportsman who inflicts injury on another player may not be the only person to incur criminal liability. Those who "aid, abet, counsel or procure the commission" of an offence may also commit an offence as a secondary party (see s 8 of the Accessories and Abettors Act 1861). The potential for secondary liability arising in a sporting context is likely to occur in two situations.

Presence and encouragement at the scene

In *R* v *Coney* (above), it was held that proof of mere voluntary presence at a prize-fight, without more, was prima facie, but not conclusive, evidence of aiding and abetting the principal's offence of battery. The secondary liability of the spectator will depend on proof (1) that his presence did encourage the commission of a violent offence, and (2) that he intended his presence to encourage the principal. Under the Law Commission's proposals, the organisation of an unrecognised sporting event at which the intentional or reckless infliction of injury is likely to occur, would represent a positive act of encouragement to unlawful activity and likely to lead to the organisers themselves incurring secondary liability in respect of any offences that may be committed by the participants. However, the Commission recognised potential difficulties in proving the requisite *mens rea* if it were alleged that a coach or team manager selected a player known to be violent and thereby encouraged the commission of an offence (see Law Com No 139, para 12.57). Finally, it is not inconceivable that a player who, having scored a goal, runs to opposing fans and celebrates in a provocative manner could face prosecution for secondary offences such as counselling and procuring or aiding and abetting any public disorder which may follow.

Failure to exercise control

A failure to exercise control is simply one aspect of the principle that the encouragement or assistance of the principal in the commission of the primary offence can give rise to liability if the alleged aider and abettor has the requisite *mens rea*. For example, a manager who sends out his players with an express directive to "nobble" the other side's star player commits a prima facie offence. Similarly, liability is capable of arising where a coach provides assistance and encouragement by negative rather than positive acts. Therefore, if a team manager fails to withdraw a player from a game who is known to be violent and dangerous, the former may face secondary liability for a failure to control the actions of the player if he commits an offence during the course of a match (see *Tuck* v *Robson* [1970] 1 WLR 741). As far as the writer is aware, the issue of vicarious – as opposed to secondary – liability for criminal conduct in a sporting context has not been tested by the courts in this country, but a successful claim has been brought by a basketball player in the United States on the ground that an employer failed to curb the propensity of one of its players to engage in dangerous play (see *Tomjanovich* v *California Sports Inc* No H-78-243 (SD Text 1979).

Public order offences

Crime on the field of play itself is not limited to physical assaults. The England international footballers, Terry Butcher and Chris Woods, were both convicted of assault which constituted a breach of the peace arising out of a fracas in an "old-firm" derby between Celtic and Rangers (see *Butcher* v *Jessop* [1989] SLT 593). During the writing of this book, Mark Bosnich, the Aston Villa goalkeeper, was seen giving a Nazi salute to Tottenham Hotspur fans who had been barracking him during a match at Tottenham's White Hart Lane ground. Such a gesture constituted a prima facie breach of section 5 the Public Order Act 1986 (which is discussed in more detail in chapter 7). Whether the sign was given in knowledge of the fact that Tottenham has a large Jewish following is unclear – it appears to have been a reference to Jurgen Klinsmann, a German national, and former Tottenham player – but Bosnich's swift declaration of contrition was not enough to save him from an FA disciplinary committee and a hefty fine although he did escape a formal prosecution.

Even more recently, the long-running feud between Arsenal's Ian Wright and Peter Schmeichel, the Manchester United goalkeeper, spilled over in a league match at Highbury amid allegations of racists remarks which Schmeichel is alleged to have made, and the physical retribution exacted by Wright. The media attention was intense, prompting a police investigation into the allegation. The outcome of those inquiries and the FA's attempts to encourage a public reconciliation between the two players remains to be seen. The incidents referred to underline the fundamental point that whilst in certain respects the law makes allowances for sport, there is no question of sporting fields being islands of immunity where competitors are entitled to disobey the laws of the land. At the professional level, there is also undoubtedly an element of the exposure which offers players such high rewards "biting them back" when they step out of line. The blow-by-blow coverage of sport from every conceivable camera angle means that it is highly unlikely that offensive words, gestures or behaviour directed at a bank of opposing fans will go unnoticed. However, the prosecuting authorities seem remarkably shy about taking action against players, particularly footballers, who engage in such unacceptable behaviour.

In this context, it should be noted that a whole raft of legislative measures has been introduced in recent years to control the behaviour of football supporters. That legislation, together with provisions intended to protect legitimate spectators, can be found in Chapter 8.

Corruption

Reference should also be made to an area of the criminal law which, thankfully, has only fleetingly touched sport in this country, but which has been brought to the fore very recently by two highly publicised cases. In the early 1960s several successful prosecutions were brought under the Prevention of Corruption Act 1906 against players for attempting to "fix" matches, and, in one case, against an agent for offering bribes to players. The penalties ranged from fines to custodial sentences. In each case, the sanctions imposed by the courts were supplemented by the FA with a *sine die* ban from playing football, or being involved in football management. The recent transfer "bung" scandal involving George Graham did not result in criminal proceedings, but Graham was banned from football management for 12 months, having already been dismissed by Arsenal despite presiding over an unprecedented period of success in the club's history. Additionally, at the time of writing, a number of defendants, including the footballers Bruce Grobelaar, John Fashanu and Hans Segers, are awaiting a second trial of allegations that they took bribes to fix Premier League matches at the instigation of Far East betting syndicates. It should be noted that match *predicting*, whilst not illegal per se, is proscribed by the FA and will almost certainly lead to disciplinary action being taken against those who participate in such an activity. Segers' defence is that he was engaged in predicting, as opposed to fixing, match results.

Disciplinary measures

The vast majority of incidents which involve a breach of the laws of a particular game are dealt with internally, without recourse to the courts. For example, a professional footballer who punches an opponent in an off-the-ball incident is likely to be disciplined by his club and the FA. At amateur level (*e.g.* a Sunday football league), disciplinary measures are likely to be regulated by an association rather than at club level. Whatever the internal structures of the game, the fact that a player is disciplined by his club and/or the body responsible for administering the particular sport does not prevent the aggrieved party from invoking the laws of the land. That is illustrated by the case of *R v Bishop* (above) where a rugby player punched an opponent during the course of a club game. The incident went unnoticed by the referee and the defendant's club failed to take disciplinary action against him. The game's governing body, the Welsh Rugby Union, suspended him, but that did not prevent him from being prosecuted for, and pleading guilty to, an offence of common assault. A one-month term of imprisonment was imposed, although the sentence was suspended on appeal. The same fate befell the Manchester United footballer Eric Cantona for his infamous kung-fu kick on a spectator at Selhurst Park (see *R v Cantona* (1995) *The Times*, 24 March). The harsh disciplinary measures which were meted out by both his club and the FA were not enough to prevent a prosecution and conviction for assault. Once again, an immediate custodial sentence was reduced on appeal, this time to a community service order.

Criminal Injuries Compensation Authority

A discussion of the scheme run by the Criminal Injuries Compensation Authority (formerly the Criminal Injuries Compensation Board) to compensate victims of crimes of criminal violence, is contained in Chapter 11.

Chapter 5

The Field of Play – Part II

Civil liability on and off the field of play

Introduction

> "By engaging in a sport ... the participants may be held to have accepted risks which are inherent in that sport ...: but this does not eliminate all duty of care of the one participant to the other." (per Barwick CJ in *Rootes* v *Shelton* [1968] ALR 33).

The above statement encapsulates the issues which this chapter seeks to address. In particular there are three matters which the reader will have to grapple with in this area: namely (1) whether a duty of care exists in the particular circumstances of a case; (2) if so, what the appropriate standard of care is; and (3) how the issue of consent affects both the nature and extent of the duty. The existence of a common law duty of care in negligence is capable of arising in a number of ways in a sporting context, but the standard may vary according to the nature of the relationship. First, this chapter looks at the duty which the participants in a sporting activity owe to one another, principally in the context of those sports where an element of physical contact is permitted by the rules of the game. The duty owed by participants to spectators is then considered, followed by the relationship between organisers of sporting events and participants on the one hand, and organisers and spectators on the other. The chapter concludes with a detailed look at the recent decision in *Smoldon* v *Whitworth and Nolan* (1996) *The Times*, 18 December and the implications which it could have for referees and other officials who are charged with the responsibility for controlling sport.

Player against player

The case frequently cited as the modern exposition of the law of negligence in the context of a sporting activity is *Condon* v *Basi* [1985] 1 WLR 866. The plaintiff was an amateur footballer who broke his leg in a tackle during a local league match. His negligence claim against the opposing player succeeded both at first instance and in the Court of Appeal. Lord Donaldson MR cited with approval the statements of the law made by the High Court of Australia in the case of *Rootes* v *Shelton* (above). The then Master of the Rolls expressed surprise that there was no authority as to the standard of care applicable to the conduct of players in competitive sports and, in particular, those sports whose rules contemplate physical contact between competitors. He identified two possible approaches in that case which, as he viewed it, had an identical effect:

(1) to take a more generalised duty of care and to modify it on the basis that the participants in the sport impliedly consent to taking risks which would otherwise be a breach of the duty of care;

(2) alternatively, that there is a general standard of care – the so-called "neighbour principle" propounded by Lord Atkin in *Donoghue* v *Stevenson* [1932] AC 562. In other words, a player is under a duty to take all reasonable care, taking into account the circumstances in which he is placed.

Lord Donaldson noted that the circumstances in which a player finds himself whilst playing a game of football are quite different to those affecting someone when they go for a walk in the country. He went on to stress that whilst the standard of care is objective, a higher standard of care may be expected from certain persons and, by way of example, stated that a higher standard was required of a player in a top flight football match than of a player in a local league match.

In the context of professional sport, the recent case of *Elliot* v *Saunders and Liverpool FC* (unreported) 10 June 1994; *Halsbury's Laws of England* 1994, *Annual Abridgement*, para 2056) achieved a high profile when it was heard in the High Court. The plaintiff and the first defendant were professional footballers playing in the Premier League, and the latter was employed by the second defendant. The plaintiff suffered a serious injury to his knee following a tackle by the second defendant and his career ended prematurely as a consequence. In his judgment, Drake J cited *Condon* v *Basi* and followed that part of the judgment of Lord Donaldson where he referred to *Rootes* v *Shelton*.

However, Drake J doubted the correctness of Lord Donaldon's theory that a higher standard of care applied to professional players. In the course of his judgment he said:

"The fact that the players are top professionals with very great skills, is no doubt one of the circumstances to be considered, but in my judgment the fact that the game is in the Premier League rather than at a lower level, does not necessarily mean that the standard of care is different."

He concluded that a deliberate foul or an error of judgment might be capable of giving rise to liability – the former, it is suggested, probably would – but, ultimately, each case turned on its own particular facts.

Since *Condon* v *Basi* is Court of Appeal authority, Lord Donaldson's statement of the law ought to take precedence over the views expressed by Drake J. A variable standard of care is applicable in other areas of the law, most notably the medical profession where a higher standard is expected of a consultant surgeon than a general practitioner who does not profess any higher calling. However, the higher level of skill displayed by professional footballers does not necessarily mean that they are any less likely to misjudge tackles than those who frequent windswept public parks on a Sunday morning. The additional ingredient is, of course, that professional footballers are constantly being judged by their performance in what is a highly competitive and short-lived career. The so-called "professional foul" is the most obvious manifestation of the win-at-all-costs philosophy and, whilst recent initiatives by the game's governing bodies have arguably reduced the incidence of foul play, the pressure to ensure that a tackle is won inevitably increases the risk of injury. In contrast, bad injuries in amateur football are often caused by clumsiness as opposed to a ruthless desire to win.

Furthermore, if Lord Donaldson is right, and the standard of care does vary according to the level at which the particular game is played, does the semi-professional or good amateur footballer owe a higher duty than a park player, but a lower duty than that owed by a Premier League player? If so, how does one articulate the semi-professional's duty in order to draw the necessary distinction? If Lord Donaldson's reasoning is followed to its logical conclusion, its practical effect is that when a Premier League side plays a non-league side in an FA Cup match, the players of the former side owe a higher standard of care to their opponents than the corresponding obligation. The simple response to that anomalous position is that since *Condon* was a case involving amateur players, Lord Donaldson's comments regarding the standard of care to be expected of a professional were *obiter*.

The rationale of *Condon* can also be criticised in other respects. First, the case of *Rootes* v *Shelton*, on which the judgment in *Condon* relies heavily, involved a water skiing accident (*i.e.* a non-contact sport). There is considerable force in the argument that the standard of care is different between contact and non-contact sports, since the risk of injury is inevitably more foreseeable in the former than the latter. Ultimately, a balancing exercise has to be carried out. On the one hand, there is the level of risk involved, the purpose of the activity, and the cost and practicability of precautions. On the other hand, the point has already been made in the context of criminal liability that the social utility of the activity in question is an important consideration when determining the appropriate standard of care in a given case. Sport is regarded as both a socially acceptable and beneficial activity, despite the increased risk of injury. Accordingly, in contact sports the standard of care is arguably lower than the ordinary standard in negligence established in *Donoghue* v *Stevenson* (above). Allied to that point, the Court of Appeal in *Condon* did not consider all the relevant authorities in this area of the law, including, *inter alia*, *Wooldridge* v *Sumner* [1963] 2 QB 43 (discussed below). In *Wooldridge* the Court of Appeal held that in the context of an injury to a spectator alleged to have been caused by the negligence of a participant, liability would only be founded if it was shown that there had been a reckless disregard for the spectator's safety. If that is the appropriate standard of care as between player and spectator, it begs the question: how can a player owe any greater duty to his fellow player, especially in a contact sport?

The decision in *Wooldridge* has had its fair share of detractors, the criticism being that it creates a special category of negligence; and there is certainly less justification for departing from ordinary principles of negligence in the context of the participant/spectator relationship. However, as between player and player, it is suggested that the "reckless disregard" test reflects the unique position which sport occupies. It has been applied in foreign jurisdictions where negligence was alleged by one player against another, notably the United States (see *e.g. Nabozny* v *Barnhill* 334 NE 2d 258 (Illinois Appellate Court 1975)). It is certainly arguable, therefore, that as between the participants in a particular sporting activity, a lower standard of care than the ordinary duty to take care is appropriate, and that the standard is the same irrespective of whether the participants are professional or amateur. In the recent case of *Smoldon* v *Whitworth and Nolan* (1996) *The Times*, 18 December the Court of Appeal expressly rejected the *Wooldridge* formulation of the duty of care, but that was in the context of a claim against a referee.

Whatever the correct state of the law may be, it was not until very recently that a court ruled in favour of a plaintiff who claimed that he had been the victim of a negligent tackle. Earlier cases had settled out of court, such as John O'Neill's claim against John Fashanu and his then club, Wimbledon. O'Neill, a Norwich City player and Northern Ireland international, was forced to retire when he ruptured knee ligaments in a challenge by Fashanu in a match in 1987. O'Neill accepted £70,000 after he agreed to withdraw an allegation of assault and battery. There was also no admission of liability on Fashanu's part. There have also been substantial out-of-court settlements in favour of Danny Thomas, the former Tottenham Hotspur player, and in 1993, Ian Durrant, the Glasgow Rangers player, accepted £225,000 plus his legal expenses the day before his action against Aberdeen Football Club and their former player, Neil Simpson, was due to be heard.

The significant breakthrough, in terms of a court ruling, was made recently when an award estimated to be in the region of £250,000 was made to a former Stockport County player, Brian McCord, whose career ended when he broke his leg in a tackle. Kennedy J found that the Swansea City player, John Cornforth, had been negligent when he challenged McCord for a loose ball in a game in March 1993. The court ruled that the tackle, in which Cornforth slid on one leg with his right foot over the ball as the pair went for a 50-50 ball, was "an error which was inconsistent with his taking reasonable care towards his opponent". The judge observed that:

> "... it does not follow that those who play football do not consent to the risk of injury. There are very few professional footballers who assert that they have never fallen below the standards expected of them and if they do they are not to be believed."

He said that he had adopted the stance that an "ordinary, reasonable" spectator would take. He could understand the many witnesses who said that the defendant had played the man rather than the ball, but that that was not his conclusion, particularly having heard his good reputation. However, he ruled that the tackle was inconsistent with taking reasonable care and it was one occasion when his skill had "deserted him" (see *McCord v Swansea City AFC* (1997) *The Times*, 11 February.

This discussion inevitably raises questions concerning the adequacy of insurance cover to protect professional sportsmen against the consequences of career-wrecking injury. Following the *Elliot* case (above), Gordon Taylor, the Chief Executive of the Professional Footballers' Association (PFA), said that the case posed a dilemma. The PFA could ignore neither a player's right to sue nor the defendant being left isolated if his club's insurers refused to take responsibility. He said that an arbitration procedure and a no-fault insurance scheme had both been considered, but had been dismissed as unworkable. Paul Elliot's claim was *not* driven by insurers seeking to cast the burden of paying his compensation onto the defendants' insurers. It was privately funded, and Elliot ended up having to pick up the substantial costs bill personally when he lost. He then had to rely on the benevolence of Chelsea's supporters to help him meet that cost by a testimonial match. One can surely be excused for thinking that that was a thoroughly unsatisfactory outcome for a fine player like Elliot, who was rightly described by Drake J as a "gentleman".

The compensation provided through the disability scheme administered by the PFA is extremely small, and with so much money passing hands in the modern professional game it is an astonishing state of affairs that more is not being done to protect its principal assets, the players. The dilemma facing Paul Elliot, like many others, is that he only had third-party insurance cover indemnifying him in respect of claims brought *against* him. Without comprehensive insurance he was exposed to the predicament which he unfortunately found himself in. He clearly needed his own personal insurance scheme, as do all other professional sportsmen and women, and advice to that effect is an essential responsibility of those involved in protecting the welfare of players. In *Smoldon* v *Whitworth* (above), Curtis J wondered whether it would not be beneficial if all players were, as a matter of general practice, to be insured, not against negligence but for the risk of catastrophic injury. In the meantime, an appropriate levy on transfer fees would surely provide an adequately large sinking fund to compensate players like Paul Elliot and Brian McCord, whose careers are blighted by injury, without the need to have recourse to law. A similar proposal was made by Lord Justice Taylor in his final report into the Hillsborough tragedy in order to provide the necessary capital for ground improvements.

Finally, where do the activities of the Up'ards and Down'ards (referred to in the Introduction) fit into the legal framework which has been discussed in this chapter and Chapter 4? The simple answer is that the participants in the game are subject to the same legal constraints which pertain in other physical contact sports. Deliberate or reckless assaults would violate the criminal law, although it could be argued convincingly that the duty of care in negligence is low.

Players and spectators

The courts have been slow to compensate spectators injured by a participant in a sporting activity which he has attended to watch. The so-called "neighbour" principle propounded by Lord Atkin in *Donoghue* v *Stevenson* (above), was applied very shortly after its formulation in the case of *Hall* v *Brooklands Auto Racing Club* [1931] 1 KB 205. There, a spectator was injured at Brooklands race track when a racing car left the track and entered the crowd. In exonerating the defendant track owners, the Court of Appeal tested their conduct by reference to concepts of reasonable care and safety.

Wooldridge v *Sumner* [1963] 2 QB 43 is perhaps the case most frequently cited for the duty which a participant owes to a spectator. The plaintiff was a photographer who was sitting close to the arena in an equestrian event when a horse ridden by the defendant went out of control and collided with him. The defendant was a skilled and experienced rider and although he was thrown in the accident he rode the horse again and it was judged to be the champion of its class. It has already been stated that the Court of Appeal held that in order to be found liable, the participant has to intend to injure the spectator deliberately, or display a reckless disregard for the safety of spectators. On the facts, the defendant was found to have simply made an error of judgment which did not amount to negligence:

> "If, in the course of a game or competition, at a moment when he has not time to think, a participant by mistake takes a wrong measure, he is not to be held guilty of any negligence" (per Diplock LJ).

In a similar vein, the Court of Appeal in *Wilks* v *Cheltenham Home Guard Motor Cycle and Light Car Club* [1971] 1 WLR 668 held that a competitor was entitled to strain himself in order to win, provided he did not act in a foolhardy manner. It should also be noted that the Court of Appeal saw the case in terms of there having been no breach of the duty of care owed by the participant to the spectator, *not* by virtue of the *volenti* principle which presupposes a tortious act. In other words, the consent which is relevant is not consent to the risk of injury but consent to the lack of reasonable care which may produce that risk. That important conceptual distinction has not always been appreciated by the courts.

Volenti non fit injuria

This is a convenient juncture to mention the general principles applicable to *volenti* in the context of torts. First, the issue does not arise until it is established that the defendant has committed a tort against the plaintiff. Secondly, a defendant must show not only that a plaintiff expressly or impliedly consented to the risk of injury, but also that he accepted that he would not be able to pursue a claim in the event that he suffered injury. If the principle is to apply, the plaintiff must be aware of the risk which he is undertaking and freely consent to it. Further, it does not necessarily follow that someone accepts a risk merely because he is aware of it. Having said that, sport is in a unique position (as the statement of Barwick CJ at the very beginning of this chapter underlines). At the risk of being repetitious, participants in certain sports impliedly consent to a degree of disregard for their own safety caused by conduct which, in other social settings, may amount to negligence but which does not give rise to a breach of duty in the context of the particular sport. The authorities seem to suggest that *volenti* does not often succeed as an outright defence. Instead, the courts appear to have taken consent into account when assessing the standard of care to be demanded of a defendant in a given situation. It clearly influenced Sellers LJ in *Wooldridge* when he said at p 56):

> "... provided the competition or game is being performed within the rules ... by a person of adequate skill and competence, the spectator does not expect his safety to be regarded by the participant."

The judgments in *Hall* (above) and *Murray v Harringay Arena Ltd* [1951] 2 KB 529 suggest that similar considerations have been applied in determining the standard of care to be expected of an organiser of sporting activities. It seems to have been set at a low level in relation to motor racing, and spectators who dodge oncoming vehicles in events like the RAC Rally are likely to get even less sympathy from the courts.

In *Wooldridge* Sellers LJ considered that there would be a difference between an injury caused, for example, by a tennis ball hit, or a racket accidentally thrown into the crowd at Wimbledon during the course of a match, and a ball hit, or a racket thrown into the stands in temper or annoyance when play was not in progress. Eric Cantona's notorious kung-fu kick on a spectator is surely the most extreme example of a breach of the duty of care which participants owe to spectators (see *R v Cantona* (1995) *The Times*, 24 March).

Lord Justice Sellers does not appear to have contemplated a player deliberately throwing himself into the crowd!

Organisers of sporting activities and spectators

In addition to owing spectators a common law duty of care, the organiser of a sporting event will invariably owe his lawful invitees a statutory duty of care under the Occupiers Liability Act 1957, as well as implied contractual duties arising out of the payment and receipt of any entrance fee. The standard of care applicable to each of those causes of action is not modified to take account of the sporting context, but issues of consent and *volenti* have arisen frequently. The obvious scenario is a spectator who is injured (or killed) as a consequence of the negligent design or construction of a stand or stadium (see the claims which followed the disasters at Ibrox, Bradford and Hillsborough, discussed in Chapter 6). Indeed, one of the first cases with a sports-related theme involved the collapse of a stand at the Cheltenham Racing Festival in 1866, where many spectators were injured (see *Frances* v *Cockrell* [1870] LR 5 QB).

A more contemporary statement of the law relating to the position of the occupier of premises where a sporting activity is being held can be found in *Murray* v *Harringay Arena Ltd* (above) and, more recently, *Wilks* v *Cheltenham Home Guard Motorcycle and Light Car Club* (above). In both those cases the claims failed. In *Wilks*, spectators who were injured at a motor cycle scramble sued the competitors involved in the accident as well as the organisers of the meeting. The Court of Appeal found that the accident was almost inexplicable. A similar finding underpinned a successful defence in *Murray* where an ice-hockey puck hit a young boy sitting at the side of an ice rink. As a general observation, spectators have not fared well with claims against organisers of sporting activities, except for the notable exception of the "disaster" cases.

Organisers, players and third parties

There have been several notable cases where members of the public in the vicinity of a sporting activity (*i.e.* persons other than participants or spectators) have either sustained injury or suffered damage to their property as a result of the activity. Once again, this begs the question: what is the nature of the duty owed to such persons? In this regard, liability is capable of arising both in negligence and nuisance. For example, inhabitants of properties living close to sporting venues are sometimes affected by the activities carried on in them. If there has been an unreasonable interference with the reasonable use and enjoyment of land, an action will lie in private nuisance. People who are affected but who do not have a sufficient interest in the land affected would have to sue in public nuisance or negligence. The primary remedy which such a person will usually seek is an injunction restraining the activity from continuing, which will often have serious implications for a club's activities. However, a defendant may argue that damages should be awarded in lieu of an injunction. In *Shelfer* v *City of London Electric Lighting* [1895] 1 Ch 287 the Court of Appeal expressed the view that the discretion to award damages in lieu of an injunction should only be exercised where the nuisance was "trivial and occasional". It was also said that the fact that a tortfeasor is in some sense a public benefactor is never a sufficient reason for refusing to grant an injunction to an individual whose rights are being persistently infringed.

In a sporting context, the plaintiff in *Bolton* v *Stone* [1951] AC 650 alleged both negligence and nuisance when she was struck by a cricket ball as she stood in a road adjoining a cricket ground. There was evidence that balls had occasionally been hit out of the ground in the past (between six and 10 times over a period of 35 years), but that nobody had been injured. The House of Lords took into account factors such as the distance of the pitch from the edge of the ground, the upward slope of the ground, and the presence of a seven-foot-high fence, and concluded that the risk of injury to someone in the plaintiff's position was so small that the defendant club had not been negligent in failing to take additional precautions such as erecting a higher fence. It was also held that no nuisance had been committed. By contrast, in the Scottish case of *Lamond* v *Glasgow Corporation* [1968] SLT 291, the occupier of a golf course was held liable in negligence for a head injury sustained by a pedestrian who was struck by a golf ball as he walked along a public lane adjoining the course. Although there had been no previous accidents, the evidence showed that some 6,000 shots were played over the fence each year, thus giving rise to a reasonably foreseeable risk of someone being hit.

The ruling in perhaps the most celebrated village cricket club case, *Miller* v *Jackson* [1977] QB 966, appears to be inconsistent with the rationale of *Shelfer*. In *Miller* a majority of the Court of Appeal declined to grant an injunction against the defendant cricket club, despite a finding that cricketers were guilty of both negligence and nuisance when they hit sixes which landed in the gardens of neighbouring properties, thus preventing the owners from using their gardens during matches. Lord Denning and Cumming-Bruce LJ concluded that the interests of the inhabitants of a village in recreation should prevail over those of the plaintiffs in the interest of their property. Although the Court of Appeal in *Miller* did decide that it was no defence to the nuisance claim that the cricket ground only became a nuisance when the plaintiff built a house close by, it is difficult to extract any true rationale on the injunction issue from the judgments in the case.

Miller was followed by *Kennaway* v *Thompson* [1981] QB 88, where the principles established in *Shelfer* were reaffirmed and applied by a differently constituted Court of Appeal. The defendant was a water-sports club whose activities were motorboat racing and water skiing. In 1972 the plaintiff moved into a house which had been built for him near the lake where the club's activities had been enjoyed since the early 1960s. After the plaintiff moved into the house, the club's activities increased in frequency, including international meetings which attracted large powerboats, with a consequential increase in the level of noise. At first instance, the plaintiff only recovered damages, Mais J refusing an injunction on the ground that to prevent the club from continuing its activities would be contrary to public interest. The Court of Appeal allowed the plaintiff's appeal and granted an injunction, ruling that the public interest should not prevail over the private interest of someone affected by a continuing nuisance (although the injunction against the defendant was in specific terms and did not represent a complete ban on its activities).

The latest in the long line of "cricket ball cases", *Lacey* v *Parker and Boyle (sued on behalf of Jordans Cricket Club)* (1994) *The Times*, 15 May, culminated in His Honour Judge Hague QC declining to grant a mandatory injunction to erect a 25-foot-high fence in front of the plaintiff's house on a picturesque village green in order to prevent cricket balls from entering his garden. The judge observed:

> "When the plaintiff bought his house he must have realised that cricket balls would occasionally intrude into his garden ... If he did not realise that, he certainly should have done."

That approach is consistent with the views expressed by Cumming-Bruce LJ in *Miller*, who concluded that no injunction should be granted against the defendant on the grounds of public interest and because the plaintiff came to the nuisance. Conversely, in *Kennaway* it was held to be no defence that the plaintiff had moved to the nuisance. Moreover, since *Miller* and *Kennaway* were decided it has been said that it would not be appropriate to deny specific private rights in order to confer indefinite advantages on the public (see *Elliott* v *Islington London Borough Council* (1991) 10 EG 145). The difficulty in discerning any consistent line of reasoning on the injunction issue from the judgments in *Miller*, a fact which was recognised by the Court of Appeal in *Kennaway*. Accordingly, there is some force in the argument that the decision in *Miller* was given *per incuriam* and should not now be followed.

Finally, in this section, *Bolton* v *Stone* was cited in the Scots law case of *Gillon* v *Chief Constable of Strathclyde Police and another* (1996) *The Times*, 22 November. The plaintiff was a police sergeant who was injured whilst undertaking crowd control duties at a football match. She was standing with her back to the pitch when a player careered into her, propelling her some distance and into a barrier. She sued her employer, claiming that she should have been warned to keep one eye on the pitch in the interests of personal safety. Lord Johnston considered that the accident was foreseeable, but that the risk was so small as not to warrant a reasonable person to take any precautions (*i.e.* applying the reasoning in *Bolton*). Her claim that the home club should have erected a barrier between the pitch and the track where she had been standing also failed since there was no evidence that barriers were in use at other clubs and they might cause dangers to spectators. Of course, a finding in favour of the pursuer (the plaintiff) against the club would have flown in the face of the main recommendation in Lord Justice Taylor's final report on the Hillsborough disaster. By the time *Gillon* was heard, football clubs had spent the previous six or seven years dismantling barriers. They could hardly be found negligent for failing to have them in place. Ultimately, the balancing exercise between the two competing risks came down heavily in favour of safeguarding the interests of the many spectators, in preference to the slight risk of a player colliding with an individual.

Liability of organisers for the actions of spectators

Two cases illustrate how successful claims can be made against the owner/occupier of a sporting venue for the acts of other visitors to its ground. First, where a plaintiff sustained personal injuries when he was knocked to the ground and trampled on by a crowd of unruly supporters who had made a deliberate and concerted attack on a gate which had given way, it was held to have been reasonably foreseeable that such a crowd might force the gate, and the occupiers of the ground were liable due to their failure to maintain the gate (see *Hosie* v *Arbroath Football Club* [1978] SLT 122).

In *Cunningham and others* v *Reading Football Club* [1991] PIQR 141 several police officers sustained personal injuries whilst they were policing a match between Reading and Bristol City. At the start of the second half, major crowd violence erupted and a pitch invasion followed. Missiles were thrown and the referee was forced to abandon the match. One police officer was struck by a large piece of concrete and was unable to defend himself when the crowd set upon him. He sustained injuries to his neck and back and also suffered post-traumatic stress disorder. There had been previous incidents involving concrete being thrown at Reading's ground, following which the club had given assurances to a Football Association inquiry that measures would be taken to avoid a repetition. However, simple and relatively cheap remedial measures were not carried out, thus providing the crowd with the ammunition used at the Bristol City match. The police officers sued Reading FC, and Drake J held the club liable. He found that the ground was appallingly dilapidated and that the club was negligent for failing to maintain it. He rejected an argument that the actions of the hooligans amounted to a *novus actus interveniens*, holding that the club ought to have known that concrete throwing was very likely to happen in the light of previous incidents.

Referees and officials

The position of officials has recently been placed under the spotlight in the case of *Smoldon* v *Whitworth and Nolan* (1996) *The Times*, 18 December, where a referee of a colts rugby union match was found liable for the very serious injuries suffered by the plaintiff as a consequence of a collapsed scrum. An opposing player was acquitted of any liability but the referee had allowed numerous scrums to collapse in what was, by all accounts, an ill-tempered match. The referee had failed to take control of the match despite warnings from his linesmen that someone would be hurt unless he took a firm grip. In dismissing the referee's appeal, the Court of Appeal ruled that the

level of care required of an official towards a player was that
appropriate in all the circumstances, taking full account of the
factual context in which he was exercising his functions as a referee.
It included his responsibility to protect the safety of the players and
to apply the rules of the game in force at the time. In the case in
question, that involved having particular regard for those rules
which were designed to minimise the acknowledged risk of serious
spinal injury resulting from a collapsed scrum. The defendant referee
had failed to take appropriate steps to prevent scrum collapse and
was liable for the foreseeable consequences of that breach of duty.

At first instance, Curtis J appears to have specifically approved of
the reasoning in *Condon* v *Basi* (although that does not emerge from
the report in *The Times* of 23 April 1996) and it is interesting to note
that in addition to *Condon*, both *Wooldridge* and *Wilks* were
referred to in the judgments of the Court of Appeal. Significantly, the
Court of Appeal concluded that the duty owed by a referee to the
players subject to his control was not the same as the one owed by
participants to spectators. In other words, a referee owes a higher
duty to the players under his control than a player does to a
spectator. It is worth looking at the arguments which were advanced
on each side and the way in which Lord Bingham, the Lord Chief
Justice, dealt with them in the leading judgment.

It was recognised at the outset that there were two competing
interests at play. On the one hand the plaintiff had been deprived of
an active and independent life, but there was also concern that the
judgment for the plaintiff would strangle a game which was enjoyed
by millions. Lord Bingham then referred to the context in which the
issues in the case arose:

- rugby was a tough, highly physical game, not for the timid or
  fragile, in which participants in serious competitive games
  could expect a fair share of knocks, bruises, strains,
  abrasions and minor bony injuries;
- the laws of the game in force during the 1991/92 season
  issued by the International Rugby Football Board and their
  accompanying instructions and notes for the guidance of
  players and referees, contained special provisions for under-
  19s. Those laws contained specific provisions for the
  protection of young players against the risk of injury caused
  by collapsed scrums. A further directive had been issued in
  March 1991 expressing concern at the continued lack of
  observance of the phased sequence of engagement of packs

within law 20(2) and requiring the strict observance of the sequence known as "crouch-touch-pause-engage" ("CTPE");

- the referee's function was to supervise the playing of the match, endeavouring to apply the rules of the game fairly and judiciously so as to ensure that the flow of play was not unnecessarily interrupted, that points awarded were fairly scored and that foul or dangerous play was discouraged and, where appropriate, penalised or prevented.

It was recognised that the referee's job often had to be performed in the context of a fast-moving, competitive and vigorous game, calling for split-second judgments and decisions. The referee could not be in all parts of the field at the same time; he could not hope to see everything that went on; it was a difficult and demanding job, usually, as here, performed out of goodwill by a devotee of the game.

The duty of care

The defendant referee based his defence on certain observations made by Sellers and Diplock LJJ in *Wooldridge* (at pp 57, 67 and 68) and argued that while he owed a duty of care and skill, nothing short of a reckless disregard for the plaintiff's safety would suffice in order to establish a breach of that duty. The plaintiff relied on the observations of Lord Donaldson in *Condon* v *Basi* to the effect that the duty was to exercise such degree of care as was appropriate in all the circumstances (*i.e.* a higher duty than that applied in *Wooldridge*). The referee contended that if the plaintiff's test were accepted, the threshold of liability would be too low, and those in the referee's position would be too vulnerable to law suits by injured players. The Court of Appeal declined to accept that that fear was well founded, and ruled that Curtis J had been correct to accept the plaintiff's formulation as the appropriate standard of care.

According to Lord Bingham, the level of care required was that which was reasonable in all the circumstances, and the circumstances were of crucial importance. The referee could not be properly held liable for errors of judgment, oversight or lapses of which any referee might be guilty in the context of a fast-moving and vigorous context. The threshold of liability was high and would not easily be crossed. He said there was no inconsistency between that conclusion and the one reached in the *Wooldridge* and *Wilks* cases, since the position of a referee *vis-a-vis* the players was not the same as that of a participant *vis-a-vis* a spectator. One of the referee's responsibilities was to safeguard the players' safety. Therefore, although the legal duty was the same, its practical content differed according to the quite different circumstances.

Causation

It was also submitted on behalf of the referee that the injury to the plaintiff had not been caused by him directly, but as a result of acts and omissions on the part of others, namely the opposing members of the scrum. Accordingly, he argued that he could not be held liable unless the court found that there was a high level of probability of injury of the kind which the laws were designed to prevent as a result of a collapsed scrum. The Court of Appeal rejected that submission and, in finding that the referee had fallen below the standard of a reasonably competent referee in his control of the scrummages in the game, pointed to the following facts and matters:

- there could be no doubt that the scrummaging rules were designed to minimise the risk of spinal injuries caused in collapsing scrums, a risk of which those managing or coaching rugby teams or refereeing or playing in matches were well aware by October 1991;
- it was accepted that the referee owed the plaintiff a duty of care and skill and that serious spinal injury was a foreseeable consequence of a scrum collapse and of failure to prevent such a collapse;
- if the referee were properly found to be in breach of his duty of care by failing to take appropriate steps to prevent a scrum collapse and if, as a result of his failure, a scrum did collapse and a player suffered spinal injuries of the kind which the rules were designed to prevent, then the referee would be liable in law for that foreseeable result of his breach of duty, despite the fact that, quantified statistically, it was a result that was very unlikely to occur;
- the evidence at trial had been that the scrums were repeatedly coming together in a rushed way and with excessive force; those impacts were the likely cause of a large majority of the scrums collapsing and that the number of impact collapses had been abnormally high. Although no finding as to the precise number of such collapsed scrums was made, there had been at least 20;
- there was clear evidence that the referee had not insisted on the CTPE sequence being followed during the match and that it had not been followed; and

- the referee's own expert had explained the difficulty for a referee in spotting who was collapsing a scrum, but that recent law changes in 1991 had given referees of colts matches the power they needed to stop scrums collapsing, and that the referee in such games was under an active duty to do so. In the expert's opinion, the referee's responsibility was to ensure that the players did not injure themselves or others, and that if the CTPE sequence was properly applied with evenly matched packs, he would not expect as many as five to six collapsed scrums. If there were 25 collapsed scrums, that would indicate that the referee's standard of refereeing was below an acceptable standard.

Volenti non fit injuria

In the alternative to the defence that he had not been negligent, the referee pleaded the defence of *volenti non fit injuria*, claiming that the plaintiff had consented to the risk of injury of the type he had sustained by voluntarily playing in the front row and/or participating in the practice of collapsing scrums, thereby increasing the risk that the opposing front row might similarly follow. The Court of Appeal held that the judge had rightly rejected that defence. The plaintiff had consented to the ordinary incidents of a game of rugby football of the kind in which he was taking part. However, given that the rules were framed for the protection of him and other players in the same position, he could not possibly be said to have consented to a breach of duty on the part of the official, whose duty it was to apply the rules and ensure that they were observed. If the plaintiff had been identified as the prime culprit in causing the collapse then that defence, and contributory negligence, might call for consideration. That was not the case.

Has the decision in *Smoldon* opened the floodgates?

At first instance, Curtis J was at pains to point out that the case was decided on its own peculiar facts and that there were certain other factors which set it apart. In the judge's view, the risk of a deluge of claims against referees should not follow provided all concerned appreciated how difficult it was for a plaintiff to establish that a referee failed to exercise the care and skill to be reasonably expected of him in the context of a hotly contested game of rugby football.

Despite that plea, one suspects that the case will encourage others to sue referees in addition to, or instead of, those who are alleged to have been directly responsible for the infliction of an injury. For instance, a boxer who suffers serious injury due to a referee's failure to stop a bout when the boxer had been displaying a clear inability to properly defend himself for several rounds, and had taken unnecessary punishment as a consequence, may attempt to sue the referee for failing to protect him and, if appropriate, for not seeking the advice of a ringside doctor.

Coaches

The survival of countless sporting clubs in this country depends on the services of unpaid volunteers who give up their spare time to supervise and coach. It would be a seriously retrograde step if that volunteer force took fright at the outcome of cases such as *Smoldon* and withdrew their priceless services. Regrettably, the blame culture which is now endemic in our society means that they should also beware. The general legal position is that if an agent offers advice to another, he owes the person(s) to whom the advice is given a duty of care to exercise the level of skill and care to be reasonably expected of him in the circumstances (see *Chaudry* v *Prabhakar* [1988] 3 All ER 718).

A professional coach could therefore be sued in negligence (and for breach of contract if he received remuneration for his services) as a consequence of negligent advice given, or techniques taught, as part of a training regime. For example, if a radical change in a professional golfer's swing results in a complete loss of form and confidence, his coach might be exposed to liability, particularly if the change was instigated by him. A less extreme example occurred on the England cricket team's winter tour to South Africa in 1995 when attempts were made to alter the bowling action of the fast-bowler Devon Malcolm. Bitter recriminations between Malcolm and the England team management followed, and the player was not picked for his country until very recently (although litigation has not ensued). A failure to reach a particular level of achievement or earnings would not be actionable unless an express undertaking or other binding promise to that effect was given by the coach. If no such obligation exists, any contract between a player and coach should say so in terms (although attempts to exclude liability for personal injury or death will fall foul of section 2 of the Unfair Contract Terms Act 1977).

As far as amateur coaches are concerned, it seems safe to assume that the ordinary common law duty in negligence will apply, although someone who holds himself out as having a particular skill or qualification when he is not entitled to make such a claim may well assume the standard of care to be expected of a trained coach, not simply the standard applied to the well-meaning amateur. Support for that theory can again be derived from the law relating to the medical profession where a general practitioner can, in certain circumstances, assume a higher duty of care towards his patient. As a general observation, coaches at all levels should acquaint themselves with developments in training techniques and equipment. It may also be necessary for coaches and instructors to acquire an appropriate level of medical knowledge. Indeed, it is arguable that such knowledge is required at most levels of instruction. For example, training with weights transcends a multitude of sporting activities and involves considerations of safe loads, limits, and the effects of fatigue. An athlete's dietary requirements may also have to be taken into account. A failure to take proper account of some, or all, of those factors, which results in injury, may well give rise to liability. A prudent coach, familiar with those requirements, would be well-advised to maintain some kind of permanent record in which advice, recommendations and training regimes are kept.

Referees and supporters

Finally, there is an interesting postscript to the *Smoldon* case. After Chelsea and Leicester had played 115 goalless minutes of their FA Cup Fifth round replay at Stamford Bridge in February 1997, it was perhaps inevitable that if a Chelsea player fell in the Leicester penalty area the home fans would cry for a penalty as the only likely way in which a goal was going to be scored in normal time. Therefore, when the Chelsea defender, Erland Johnsen, duly obliged and the referee, Mike Reed, reciprocated by awarding a highly dubious penalty, Chelsea took their chance and progressed into the next round. The righteous indignation of the Leicester manager, Martin O'Neill, at the injustice which had been perpetrated against his team was bettered, shortly afterwards, by proceedings issued against the hapless Mr Reed by some Leicester supporters who claimed compensation for the severe distress and anxiety which they allegedly suffered as a consequence of his decision, compelling them to take time off work in order to recover from the psychological trauma!

At the time of writing, the litigation is still afoot (at least, to the best of the author's knowledge) and it would therefore be inappropriate to pass any comment on the merits of the case. Presumably, however, the small matter as to the existence, or otherwise, of a duty of care on the part of the referee towards many thousands of spectators for his decisions will be ventilated sooner rather than later, as will the issues of breach, foreseeability and causation. Nevertheless, with the massive financial rewards available in modern sport, the day may come when a club sues an official for an allegedly negligent decision which terminates a lucrative cup run prematurely, or ends a side's title chances. Such a claim would obviously be fraught with difficulties, but if supporters are willing to invest in similar litigation, is the prospect of a club following suit so far-fetched?

Chapter 6

Schools, Local Authorities and Other Organisers

Introduction

The legal position of schools, local authorities and clubs, and the duties and obligations conferred upon them by the law, requires separate consideration but, as they share certain common features, it is convenient to discuss them together in one place. The courts have been called upon to adjudicate on negligence actions brought against schools and teachers for accidents involving pupils since the 1930s. If the reported cases are representative, the principal complaint levelled at schools is a failure properly to supervise games activities. The recent introduction of criteria enabling teachers to assess the level of risk involved in a particular activity should, if rigorously applied, reduce the incidence of games-related injuries in schools. Actions against local authorities may also involve an alleged failure to provide adequate training or instruction, or to supervise an activity. However, it is the condition of premises and equipment provided by local authorities which has often proved to be a council's "Achilles Heel". Outside those two categories, organised sports and recreational activities range from five-a-side football tournaments to orienteering courses. Specialist activities also occupy a small niche in the holiday market. The Lyme Bay canoeing tragedy has concentrated the minds of both Parliament, and the organisers of outdoor activities, on the importance of safeguarding the health and welfare of participants, who are frequently of school age.

Schools

Introduction

The importance of physical education in our overall development, which was recognised by the courts as long ago as 1915 in *Re Mariette* [1915] 2 Ch 384, is underlined by its inclusion as a core subject in the National Curriculum (see the Education (National Curriculum) (Attainment Targets and Programmes of Study in Physical Education)

Order 1995 (SI 1995/60)). The core elements of the Order, which should be read in conjunction with the HMSO publication *Physical Education in the National Curriculum*, target risk assessment, risk monitoring and risk minimising, a sequence which reflects the demands of European Law and the scheme of the new health and safety regulations which were introduced on 1 January 1993 (the so-called "six pack"). The concepts of programmes of study (POS) and end of key stage statements (EKSS) are designed to assist the teaching profession in assessing whether a particular activity is suitable for a particular age group. At present, the key stages are: 1 (five to eight years); 2 (eight to 11 years); 3 (11 to 14 years); and 4 (14 to 16 years). Guidance is given as to which sports are appropriate for which age band and, the level of risk involved in a particular activity should be assessed by reference to a number of criteria, including the teacher's experience and qualifications, pupil development and attitudes, the nature and condition of the equipment required for the activity, and even the climate. By attaching appropriate weight to each factor, a judgment can be made as to whether the overall risk in a particular activity is high, medium or low.

In practice, those involved in teaching games and sport in schools should acquire an ability to train and instruct pupils in the basic skills of a game or sport, together with the safe use of equipment and other games facilities. Those requirements should be underpinned by pupils acquiring a knowledge of, and respect for, the rules of the game, principles of fair play and sportsmanship, and respect for other participants. Schools and teachers ignore the acquisition of such skills at their peril, since it is well established that in certain circumstances schools and, where appropriate, the education authorities responsible for their management and control, can be liable in damages for personal injuries sustained by their pupils whilst participating in sport or play. That liability is concurrent with the personal liability of the teacher or other member of staff who is alleged to have been directly responsible for a negligent act or omission. Once again, the existence of a duty of care is beyond dispute. A teacher stands in *loco parentis* to his pupils and owes them a duty to exercise reasonable care for their health and safety (*i.e.* a broader duty than the one contended for by the author as between participants). The question to be asked is: what would one have expected of a reasonable and prudent parent in the same position as the teacher?

Although there is no legal requirement for a teacher to hold any specific qualification for teaching sport or physical education, there will be instances where a well-meaning amateur may expose himself and his employer to liability. Certain sports, such as archery and field sports which carry inherent risks, should only be taught or supervised by those with relevant training (see *e.g. Liversidge* v *Central Regional Council* (1983) (unreported) where a teacher was qualified in martial arts but was not a qualified instructor). Similarly, teachers (or any other adult for that matter) should only supervise swimming classes if they are practised in emergency procedures. Guidance on the above and other related matters can be obtained from the British Association of Advisers and Lecturers in Physical Education, which provides advice and assistance on all aspects of physical education. The Association produces a booklet entitled *Safe Practice in Physical Education* (Dudley Lea Publications) which is approved of and recommended by the Department for Education and Employment.

Training and instruction

It has already been stated that basic training and instruction is one of the mainstays of good teaching practice in physical education classes. Therefore, where a 14-year-old boy broke his neck when he dived off a starting block into the shallow end of a swimming pool, he succeeded in an action against the teacher for failing to instruct him how to dive safely into shallow water, and also against the Amateur Swimming Association for not giving teachers adequate warning of the dangers created by a lack of coaching knowledge (see *Gannon* v *Rotherham Metropolitan Borough Council* (1991) *Halsburys Laws* MR 91/1653). However, it will often be difficult to show that a failure properly to instruct or train, as opposed to an unforeseeable accident, caused the plaintiff's injuries, especially in sports where physical contact is permitted by the rules of the game. That was one of the grounds on which the claim in *Van Oppen* v *The Clerk to the Trustees of the Bedford Charity (Harpur Trust)* [1989] 1 All ER 273 foundered (see below).

Supervision

Cases in the 1930s showed the limits the courts were prepared to impose for a failure properly to supervise pupils participating in sporting activities. In *Langham* v *Governors of Wellingborough School and Fryer* (1932) 101 LKJB 513 a pupil hit a golf ball in a school playground which struck a fellow pupil in the eye. The evidence showed that striking golf balls in the playground was not a common occurrence and both the school and its staff were absolved from liability. The court found that such an occurrence could not have been prevented even by adequate supervision. However, whilst the case had a sporting link, the accident did not happen in the context of a dedicated games lesson.

The difficulties involved in determining whether or not the level of supervision is adequate is illustrated by two cases with remarkably similar facts, but with different outcomes. In *Gibbs* v *Barking Corporation* [1936] All ER 115, a schoolboy injured himself while attempting a vaulting exercise in a gymnastics class. The schoolmaster responsible for overseeing the activity was found to have been negligent for failing to supervise the vault and preventing the stumble which caused the boy's injury. By contrast, in *Wright* v *Cheshire County Council* [1952] 2 All ER 789 a teacher was exonerated from blame for injuries sustained by a 12-year-old boy who fell during a vaulting exercise in a school gym. There were a number of activities and the teacher moved from one to the other, leaving each group to supervise itself. The pupils in the vaulting group all had experience of the exercise but, at the sound of the school bell, the boy at the receiving end of the buck ran off before catching the plaintiff. Although a physical training instructor had been called to give evidence that the practice adopted by the teacher was dangerous, it was generally approved of and had served well in the past.

The Court of Appeal in *Wright* held that what was reasonable in everyday affairs might well be answered by experience arising out of practices which have been generally and successfully adopted for many years. *Gibbs* was distinguished on the ground that the Court of Appeal in that case had declined to upset a finding of fact made by the trial judge. However, it does not make it easy to discern a consistent principle. In the late 1990s, the courts are likely to be less tolerant of lapses in supervision, but adherence or otherwise to the requirements of the 1995 Order, together with the accompanying guidance, will presumably weigh heavily in the balance when a court is called upon to decide whether a particular failure was negligent.

Equipment and facilities

A montage of sporting "gaffes" always seems to include the hapless Daley Thompson on the occasion when his pole vault snapped in two as he prepared to jump, leaving him prostrate. Luckily, only his pride was hurt, but the incident shows how inadequate or flawed sports equipment or facilities might be capable of causing injury. In *Ralph* v *LCC* (1946) 63 TLR 546 the defendant was held liable for injuries sustained by the plaintiff schoolboy in a school game of touch which was played in a room with insufficient space. The plaintiff sustained an injury to his hand when he put it through a glass partition. The decision of the Court of Appeal was based on the premise that a reasonable and prudent father would have contemplated the possibility of such an accident. It is perhaps the most obvious example of an application of the loco parentis principle which, to all intents and purposes, places a teacher in the shoes of the child's parent.

Teacher participation in games

More recently there have been two notable cases involving sporting accidents at schools, the first involving a teacher participating in a game with his pupils. In *Affutu-Nartoy* v *Clarke and ILEA* (1984) *The Times*, 9 February a school-master was found liable for tackling a 15-year-old boy in a rugby match. The court held that the duty of care was not breached simply because the teacher took part in the game with his pupils, since that was a perfectly proper way of demonstrating non-contact skills such as passing and kicking the ball. However, he crossed the rubicon when he involved himself in the physical side of the game, since the disparity in weight, height and strength between the teacher and his pupils gave rise to a reasonably foreseeable risk of injury to the pupils. Although the point did not arise, a teacher who takes sides in a game with his pupils should satisfy himself that he will be able to maintain proper control of the game.

A duty to insure?

Parents probably pay little, if any, regard to the question whether their children are insured whilst taking part in games and sport at school. The issue arose in *Van Oppen* v *The Clerk to the Trustees of the Bedford Charity (Harpur Trust)* [1989] 1 All ER 273 (affirmed at [1989] 3 All ER 387). The schoolboy plaintiff claimed damages for alleged negligence against the trustees of his former school for serious injuries which he sustained during a house rugby match when he was 16. He alleged that the school had failed to:

(1) take reasonable care for his safety on the field of play by failing to coach or instruct him in proper tackling techniques and, in particular, the head-on tackle;

(2) ensure that he was insured against accidental injury at the time of the accident;

(3) advise his father of (a) the inherent risk of serious injury in the game of rugby; (b) the consequential need for personal accident insurance; and (c) the fact that the school had not arranged such insurance.

The claim was dismissed on all the grounds complained of. As far as the first allegation was concerned, the trial judge found on the evidence that what had happened could properly be described as "a tragic accident" due to a mistimed tackle, not by any coaching or training error, or omission.

The decision is more noteworthy for the finding that there was no duty on the part of the school to effect insurance cover. The relationship of school and pupil does not give rise to such a general duty. The third limb of the claim failed on the ground that as there is no obligation on the part of parents to insure their offspring, a school cannot be under any higher duty. That finding was made against the background of a report prepared by the Medical Officers of Schools Association in 1979 which urgently recommended that schools should take out accident insurance for pupil rugby players. Paradoxically, if an employee of the school (*e.g.* a games master) had been injured playing in the same game, any failure on the part of the school to insure him against injury would have been an offence under section 5 of the Employers' Liability (Compulsory Insurance) Act 1969 (albeit that the Act does not give rise to civil liability).

Disabled children

It should be noted that there is a clear line of authority for the proposition that a higher duty of care is owed to disabled children (and adults) than to able-bodied children (see *Morrell v Owen and others* (1993) *The Times*, 14 December).

Local authorities

Introduction

Liability on the part of local authorities for injuries sustained by those who make use of its facilities and equipment for sporting and other recreation purposes is capable of arising in a number of different ways. A typical claim will involve the alleged failure of a district or county council adequately to maintain the land or property which it owns and occupies, and where sporting activities take place, or to maintain safe and adequate equipment which it provides to members of the public to use. There is also the possibility of a local authority being vicariously liable for the torts of its employees performed in the course of their employment. Typically, claims will be brought in common law negligence and, in appropriate cases, under the Occupiers' Liability Act 1957. The usual duties of care will be applied, the relevant standard being dictated by the circumstances of each particular case. Where a fee has been made for use of a sports hall or equipment, a claim will also lie in contract, although there is often little advantage in adding that cause of action to one in negligence.

Defects in premises

A frequent scenario may be accidents which occur due to the condition of premises and, in particular, defects in the floor of a sports hall or gym. In *Gillmore* v *London County Council* [1938] 4 All ER 331 the plaintiff slipped and injured himself on a highly polished floor whilst participating in a physical exercise class. The floor was suitable for dancing, but not for the sort of activity which the plaintiff was engaged in when he injured himself. The local authority which organised the activity was found to have failed in its duty to provide a floor which was reasonably safe in the circumstances. The floor created a danger beyond the usual degree of danger involved in playing a game. A plea of *volenti* failed because of the absence of the plaintiff's consent to the additional danger, above and beyond the normal risks involved. The plaintiff paid a fee for attending the class and, if the facts were repeated today, he would have prima facie causes of action in contract, negligence, and for breach of statutory duty under the Occupiers' Liability Act 1957. The duty in *Gillmore* was couched in terms of reasonable care, but in such cases there is arguably an analogy with the law applied in the context of slipping accidents in supermarkets (see *Ward* v *Tesco Stores* [1976] 1 WLR 810 where the duty applied by the court was virtually absolute).

Like supermarkets, the floors of sports halls, squash courts etc are susceptible to spillages and deposits of sweat which can render a polished surface very slippery. Indeed, a spillage on the floor of a sports hall is apt to represent a far greater danger than a similar occurrence in a supermarket. Badminton, squash and basketball, for example, all involve short, concerted bursts of speed, with a premium placed on being able to stop and turn quickly. The dynamics of such movements impose great physical pressure, and the need to play them on a level, even and dry surface is essential. Each case will turn on its own particular facts but, it is submitted, there is a heavy burden imposed on the owners and occupiers of sports halls to implement an adequate system of inspection, maintenance and cleaning. In one such case (in which the author was involved) a leaky roof caused water to collect on the floor of a gymnasium with predictable results when the plaintiff played a game of badminton and slipped on the puddle. The discovery process, as in conventional tripping cases, can often dictate the outcome of such claims.

Supervision

As with schools, another way in which claims are frequently encountered is where it is alleged that a local authority has failed adequately to supervise a sporting event or venue, or to discharge its functions as the body responsible for implementing health and safety legislation for the area under its control. At one level, this could involve a claim that pool attendants at public swimming baths failed adequately to supervise swimmers with the result that someone is injured. In *Clark* v *Bethnal Green Corporation* (1939) 55 TLR 519 a child at a public swimming bath unexpectedly let go of a springboard from which another child was preparing to jump, thereby causing the latter child to suffer injury. The evidence clearly pointed to a lack of adequate supervision, but the claim failed on the ground that the actions of the first child were not capable of anticipation; in other words, the lack of supervision was not causative of the plaintiff's injuries. A less common occurrence might be the failure of a local authority to ensure that a football ground complied with the safety requirements relating to such venues (*e.g.* the Safety of Sports Grounds Act 1975 and the Sporting Events (Control of Alcohol etc) Act 1985, which are discussed in more detail in Chapter 8).

For those who represent defendants, a recent case limiting the liability of organisers of sporting activities is *Fowles* v *Bedfordshire County Council* (unreported) 17 May 1995, CA. The plaintiff was an accomplished gymnast who was performing a gymnastic exercise in premises owned and controlled by the defendant local authority. The exercise the plaintiff attempted to perform involved a somersault on a mat which had been placed too close to a wall. He collided with the wall, suffering serious and permanent injury. The Court of Appeal held that the defendant had assumed a duty to make the plaintiff aware of the risks involved since it had provided one of its employees who had assumed the task of teaching the plaintiff how to do somersaults. However, the plaintiff was also found to have taken insufficient care for his own safety, and his damages were reduced to reflect his contributory negligence. The significant aspect of the case is that the Court of Appeal accepted the argument that the mere provision of facilities and lack of supervision, coupled with the foreseeable risk of injury, would not have been enough to render the defendant liable. In other words, there had to be a further aggravating feature to render the local authority liable (which there was, in the form of the mat being placed too close to the wall by one of the defendant's employees).

Volenti non fit injuria

The general principles of *volenti* have already been discussed. A case which insurers of sports clubs and local authorities frequently cite is *Jones* v *Northampton Borough Council* (1990) *The Times*, 21 May which has already been referred to in the context of the duty of care owed by the members of an unincorporated association to one another. The plaintiff, Hugh Jones, was injured playing indoor football on a pitch hired from the council by a friend, Peter Owen. The latter had been informed that the roof leaked before he hired the pitch. Jones slipped on water which had settled on the pitch and sustained serious injuries. Jones sued both the council and Owen. The council settled the claim for £3,000 and then successfully claimed an indemnity from Owen under the Civil Liability (Contribution) Act 1978.

It is interesting to note that the Court of Appeal found that the council had discharged its duty to Jones by virtue of the warning which it had given to Owen. Similarly, the council was not in breach of the contract it had entered into with Owen. Since Owen had been informed of the risk, he was *volens* the same (*i.e.* he had assumed the risk that he could not recover from the council). However, the position might have been different if the players had not been members of an unincorporated association and did not owe one another a mutual duty to inform. It is suggested that Jones would have been entitled to succeed in his claim against the council for failing to bring the defect in the roof specifically to his attention, unless the council could have persuaded the court that Owen still constituted himself as agent for the other members of his party when he signed the hiring form. It is also interesting to consider whether the outcome would have been any different if, for example, a group of schoolboys had hired the pitch. In Jones, Owen and his fellow participants were adults and could make up their own minds as to whether to play on the pitch. Depending on their age, a court might not necessarily arrive at the same conclusion in relation to juveniles.

Jones was distinguished in *Dawson* v *West Yorkshire Police Authority* (reported in *Personal and Medical Injuries Law Letter*, October 1995). The plaintiff slipped in a police gymnasium whilst playing five-a-side football. He was attending a training course, although the game was not arranged as part of the course. The floor was in the process of being resurfaced and there had been previous complaints. The plaintiff was aware that the floor was slippery and had made remarks to an instructor. Despite his knowledge of the potential danger, the plaintiff's claim succeeded, the trial judge finding that he had been encouraged to take part in extra-curricular activities which would help foster camaraderie, maintain fitness and assist team building. It seems, therefore, that the judge was influenced by the fact that an element of compulsion was involved, even though the game was not technically part of the set itinerary. Another distinction between the two cases is that *Dawson* involved a claim against an employer and the duty of care was therefore higher than the ordinary duty in negligence. Within reason, an employee subordinates his freedom of choice to the will of his employer, and if the latter exposes the former to an unsafe working environment, the employer cannot later be heard to complain that the employee knew he might suffer injury. Why should a training course which involves sporting activities be treated any differently to a training course on how to use a piece of machinery?

Other organisers of sporting activities

Introduction

Outdoor activities are probably the most important example of third parties assuming responsibility for the welfare and safety of others. A common law duty of care in negligence will inevitably arise, although the contractual position may be complicated when minors are involved, particularly where payment for an activity course is made, for example, by a parent or school. In certain circumstances, specific statutory obligations are imposed on the organisers of such activities, and a corresponding benefit should accrue to those who participate. In the most extreme cases, the organisers of sporting activities can incur criminal as well as civil liability. Holidays which involve organised sporting activities are becoming increasingly popular.

The Lyme Bay tragedy

The organisers of the fateful Lyme Bay canoeing expedition on 22 March 1993 transgressed both the civil and criminal law when the activity ended in tragedy. The defendants were prosecuted for manslaughter on the basis that the four children who died were unlawfully killed due to gross negligence. The case against the managing director of the company which organised and ran the ill-fated trip was that he had primary responsibility for devising, instituting, enforcing and maintaining an appropriate safety policy. He failed both in that responsibility and in his duty to supervise the manager of the activity centre in question. It was also said against him that he employed instructors who lacked experience and who were unsuitable to lead an expedition of the kind in question. Both the company and its managing director were convicted, and the latter was sentenced to three years' imprisonment (later reduced to two years on appeal: see *R v Kite and OLL Ltd* (1994) *The Independent*, 19 December for a report of the trial between Ognall J and a jury and (1996) 2 Cr App R (S) 295 (CA). A £60,000 fine was also imposed.

In an attempt to avoid a repetition of the tragedy, Parliament has intervened with the Activity Centres (Young Persons' Safety) Act 1995. The Act regulates activity centres and the providers of facilities where children and young persons under the age of 18 engage in adventure activities. The facilities contemplated by the Act are those which consist of, or include, some element of instruction or leadership given to young persons (under the age of 18) in connection with their engagement in an adventure activity. An "adventure activity" is defined as caving, climbing, trekking or watersports.

Subordinate legislation has been introduced under the Act. The Adventure Activities (Licensing) Designation Order 1996 (SI 1996/771), which came into force on 16th April 1996, designates Tourism Statutes Limited as the licensing authority responsible for the exercise of functions relating to the licensing of persons providing adventure holiday facilities. On the same date, the Adventure Activities Licensing Regulations 1996 (SI 1996/772) were also introduced, which establish a framework for the licensing of persons who provide facilities for adventure activities. Generally, a person is required to hold a licence if he provides facilities for adventure activities in return for payment, or, being a local authority, provides such facilities to an educational establishment for the benefit of its pupils. It is now a criminal offence for a person:

(1) to do anything for which a licence is required other than in accordance with such a licence; or

(2) to make false statements to the appropriate licensing authority for the purpose of obtaining or holding a licence.

If anyone involved in sporting activity was in any doubt before, it is now clear that the employers of coaches and instructors must ensure that their employees are trained and kept up to date with such things as developments in coaching techniques and equipment. An ability to administer basic first-aid is an essential prerequisite just as it is with teachers.

The design of facilities

The design of sporting facilities may give rise to an unacceptable risk of injury, and there is no reason in principle why the legal position of schools, local authorities and others should be any different. In *Rayner* v *Center Parcs Limited* (unreported) (1994), the plaintiff dived into a leisure pool with a wave-making machine and struck his head on the bottom, fracturing his spine. As a consequence of the accident, he was confined to a wheelchair. The defendant had intended to prohibit diving into the pool as the water was only four feet deep. The plaintiff contended that there were inadequate signs to indicate that diving was prohibited. He also sought to rely on the fact that the wave-making machine obscured the true depth of the pool. The case was eventually settled with liability split equally. Recommendations concerning the safe depth of swimming pools and the height of diving boards can be obtained from FINA and the Amateur Swimming Association (see Appendix for addresses of these organisations).

Chapter 7

Spectators

Part I – Sporting catastrophes

Introduction

On 15 April 1989, 95 football fans were crushed to death and more than 400 were injured in the Hillsborough disaster, the worst sporting catastrophe this country has known in terms of loss of life. The inquiry prompted by the tragedy and the recommendations contained in the interim and final Reports of Lord Justice Taylor (as he then was) are credited, in no small part, with the rejuvenation of professional football, at least at the highest level. However, the most important consequence of the vast improvements which have been made to football stadia in this country in compliance with the Taylor recommendations appears to have been taken for granted. The increased safety in which football can now be watched accentuates the failure of successive governments and football's governing bodies to learn the lessons of previous disasters, dating as far back as 1902 when the first tragedy at the Ibrox Park ground of Glasgow Rangers FC occurred. Even earlier than that, spectators were suffering at the hands of negligent providers of facilities at sporting venues (see *Francis* v *Cockerell* (1870) 5 LRQB 501).

The first FA Cup Final at Wembley, between Bolton Wanderers and West Ham, in April 1923, will forever be remembered for the presence of the famous white horse on the pitch as police attempted to restrain a crowd in the region of 125,000. At the time, the ground had a capacity of 93,000 and although there were over 1,000 casualties, it is a miracle that no fatalities were recorded. However, such a miracle was not repeated when, one year after the end of the Second World War, 33 spectators were crushed to death in an FA Cup tie, again involving the unfortunate Bolton Wanderers, this time against Stoke City. In more recent memory, the twisted and tangled wreckage of the handrails which lined the flight of steps on which 44 spectators lost their lives at Ibrox in 1971, and the harrowing scenes of spectators trying to escape the Bradford City fire in 1985, are never-to-be-forgotten images. Three years after the second Ibrox

Disaster, the personal representatives of the deceased victims succeeded in a negligence claim against Glasgow Rangers (see *Dougan* v *Rangers Football Club* (1974) *Daily Telegraph*, 24 October). Thirteen years later Bradford City Football Club and the local fire authority were both held liable for the Bradford fire (see *Fletcher and Britton* v *Bradford City Association Football Club and others* (1987) *The Times*, 24 February).

No one could dispute that the events at Ibrox, Bradford and Hillsborough are properly described as "catastrophes" which, by their very nature and scale, have become enshrined in the public consciousness. This chapter begins with a brief look at the litigation spawned by the Hillsborough tragedy, and goes on to chart the history of the public inquiries which were ordered, and the legislation which has been introduced, in order to improve the safety of spectators at sporting events. The general legal principles relating to the liability of organisers of sporting events has already been discussed in Chapters 5 and 6.

The Hillsborough litigation

From a legal perspective, the Hillsborough disaster precipitated litigation from a variety of different sources for the admitted negligence on the part of the police. As elsewhere, there is an overlap between the legal issues involved here and those in other areas of this book. Furthermore, it should be said from the outset that the principles of law involved in the cases are of general application; the fact that the events which prompted their consideration by the courts took place in a sporting context is of no particular significance. It is a prime example of sport playing its part in the shaping and development of the law, but to talk about the "Hillsborough cases" as if they were some discrete aspect of "sports law" is fallacious. That point made, the legal principles involved are of particular importance to common lawyers, particularly personal injury practitioners. There were four classes of Hillsborough claimant: the first class comprised the estates and dependants of those who died; the second class were those who were injured in the ground, and survived; the third class were the relatives of those who died and who actually witnessed the horrific events as they unfolded inside the ground, or who saw the scenes on television and claimed to have suffered psychiatric damage as a consequence (*i.e.* so-called "nervous shock" claims); and the fourth class were members of the police and rescue services who were on duty at Hillsborough on the fateful day, and who also claimed to have suffered psychiatric injuries.

Physical injury suffered by those in the ground

Most of the cases in the first and second classes of plaintiff were the subject of out-of-court settlements, although *Hicks v Chief Constable of South Yorkshire Police* [1992] 2 All ER 65, HL, [1992] 1 All ER 690, CA was a notable exception. Those who suffered injuries in the Hillsborough and Bradford tragedies, but who survived, were, of course, entitled to be compensated for any physical injury. Those unfortunate enough to have been trapped in the crush, but who escaped without physical injury, had no claim for the distress they suffered as a result of an undeniably terrifying experience. However, where someone's life expectancy is reduced as a result of injuries sustained, the distress which the plaintiff suffers in that knowledge sounds in damages. In *Hicks* the father of two girls who suffered traumatic asphyxia and died in the crush at Hillsborough failed in his action on the ground that since unconsciousness and death occurred within such a short space of time (about five minutes), the asphyxia was effectively part of the death itself. Consequently, no damages were recoverable for the pain and suffering attributable to that brief period. Both the Court of Appeal and the House of Lords refused to go behind the findings of fact made by the trial judge which were clearly crucial to the outcome. It follows that the fear of impending death felt by the victim of a fatal injury before the infliction of that injury does not give rise to a cause of action capable of surviving for the benefit of the deceased's estate. Ultimately, the claim in *Hicks* failed because the plaintiffs failed to discharge the burden of proving that the deceased had suffered any physical injury prior to the fatal crushing injury which caused their deaths (although doubts have recently been expressed regarding the findings made by the coroner in that regard).

Psychiatric damage suffered by relatives

None of the claimants in the third and fourth categories suffered physical injuries and the issues of law applicable to those claims arose solely out of psychiatric damage suffered as a consequence of witnessing the horrific events (so-called "nervous shock" cases). As far as the third class of claimant was concerned, the first hurdle the plaintiffs had to overcome was to show that they had suffered recognisable psychiatric trauma over and above the ordinary feelings of grief and distress which one would normally expect to experience at the death of a loved one. A diagnosis of psychiatric illness, such as post-traumatic stress disorder, can now be evaluated by reference to internationally recognised standards set out in the *Classification of Mental and Behavioural Disorders* produced by the World Health Organisation (ed ICD 10, WHO Geneva, 1992). The feature which differentiates psychiatric trauma from physical injury is that it is capable of affecting a much wider range of people than just the direct victims of a defendant's negligence. Public policy reasons therefore dictate that the law should impose a limit on the number of claims which can be brought by those who claim to have suffered damage of the former nature. This is achieved by reference to a three-stage filter test:

(1) the class of persons whose claims should be recognised;
(2) the proximity of members of the class to the event in question; and
(3) the means by which the trauma is inflicted.

In *Alcock* v *Chief Constable of South Yorkshire* [1992] 1 AC 310 the House of Lords dealt with the first element by recognising that close ties of love and affection often exist outside the formal family framework, and therefore rejected any arbitrary qualification by reference to particular relationships such as husband and wife, or parent and child. The test is one of reasonable foreseeability, subject to the *caveat* that a sufficiently close relationship of affection will be readily presumed in the case of close relatives, and the claims of non-relatives should be looked at closely. Mr Alcock was in the stand at Hillsborough and lost his brother-in-law, whose body he later identified in the morgue. His claim failed, as did that of another plaintiff, Mr Harrison, who lost two brothers in the tragedy. There was found to be no evidence of particularly close ties of love and affection in either case, but the judgments of Lord Ackner and Lord Jauncey implicitly suggest that had the point been resolved in their favour, both plaintiffs would have succeeded. A further ground on which the claim in *Alcock* failed was that the delay between the accident and the sight of the bodies by the plaintiff was nine hours (*cf* the delay in *McLoughlin* v *O'Brian* [1983] 1 AC 410) and, according to Lord Jauncey, the purpose of the plaintiff's visit to hospital was to formally identify a body, as opposed to providing care and comfort.

Claims made by members of the rescue services

The class of claimants entitled to pursue claims for psychiatric damage suffered as a result of witnessing an horrific event is not restricted to relatives. In *Chadwick v British Railways Board* [1967] 1 WLR 912 a successful claim for psychiatric damage was brought by a rescuer who had no relationship with the victims. Any doubt which may have existed over whether *Chadwick* survived *Alcock* has been dispelled by the decision of the Court of Appeal in *Frost and others v Chief Constable of South Yorkshire Police and others* (1996) *The Times*, 6 November. In *Frost* liability had been admitted and damages assessed in relation to 14 police officers who had either entered the spectator pens at the Leppings Lane end of the ground (where the Liverpool fans congregated), or were involved at the pitch-side fence which enclosed the pens. As to the appellant officers, it was not disputed that they had all sustained post-traumatic stress disorder, but the defendants denied the existence of any duty to them. The roles played by the appellants represented the different types of activity performed by the remaining claimants. The four officers whose appeals succeeded all sustained psychiatric injury as a result of tending to victims of the disaster. All except one were found to be rescuers, but the fourth, who was present at the ground in the course of his duty, was exposed to the horrific events which ensued. In those circumstances, it was held that there had been a breach of the duty of care which the Chief Constable owed to him as his employer. The appeal of an officer who was employed on mortuary duties after the event was dismissed.

The decision in *Frost* has paved the way for members of the rescue services to recover damages for "nervous shock" in circumstances where relatives of the deceased might not. Taken at its face value, it is, perhaps, hardly surprising that the decision in *Frost* has been heavily criticised by the tabloid press, the media and the families of the Hillsborough victims alike. The most typical reaction from non-legal commentators has been that men and women join the police force in the knowledge that they might be called upon to assist at a major tragedy; in other words, the events at Hillsborough were a kind of occupational hazard which the plaintiffs impliedly consented to when they joined up. That position, however, overlooks the fact that policemen and women are owed a duty of care by their employer just as any other employee is. It is also well established that the standard of an employer's duty towards his employees is higher than the ordinary duty to take reasonable care. Hillsborough was untypical, in the sense that it was the employer's negligence which was responsible for creating a rescue situation.

Conversely, a mere bystander, whether a policeman or a layman, who was not a rescuer and to whom no such duty was owed by the tortfeasor, would not generally be able to recover damages and would only be able to do so if he was linked by ties of love and affection to a primary victim and otherwise fulfilled the criteria in *McLoughlin, Alcock, and Page* v *Smith* [1996] 1 AC 155. Post-*Alcock* and *Frost*, the position still appears to be that members of the emergency services are deemed to be within the reasonable contemplation of the defendant and can sue, whereas mere bystanders cannot. Henry LJ pre-empted the furore which has greeted the decision in *Frost* when he stated that whilst respecting the feelings of the relatives, a plaintiff could only recover according to the different principles of law applicable to his category. However, detractors from the decision have inevitably asked the question: does a law which allows police officers to recover, but which fails to compensate the loved ones of those who have died, have any place in a fair and just society? It is difficult not to have sympathy with the contention that the Hillsborough litigation has shown that the law in this area is out of step in its treatment of those whose lives are intimately affected by such tragedies, since it places third parties in a better position than relatives.

Part II – regulation, control and safety of spectators

Introduction

In the past 20 years or so Parliament has passed a significant body of legislation, both primary and subordinate, which is intended to regulate and control the conduct of spectators during and, in some cases, before, sporting events. It has also introduced statutory provisions designed to protect spectators and provide them with a standard of safety and comfort which was conspicuous by its absence for far too long. The initiative for this legislative activity was derived from two very different sources. First, for reasons which are beyond the scope of this book, this country has been the victim of a social malaise for over a quarter of a century, which has brought nothing but shame, censure and, ultimately, our expulsion from a number of European football competitions. The curse of the football hooligan has been less conspicuous in recent times, but one senses that it is still only being kept at arm's length, principally by improved policing and security measures at grounds. Secondly, the need to provide greater protection to spectators was clearly driven by the tragedies referred to earlier in this chapter. In his final report on the Hillsborough disaster, Lord Justice Taylor noted that it was a "truism" that safety and crowd control are interdependent, and that measures to control a crowd almost always have an impact on safety. The statutory provisions set out below seek to achieve those twin goals, and most of the legislation was introduced with the objective of addressing the specific needs of sport, principally football. Other legislation of more general application, such as the Occupiers' Liability Act 1957 and the Public Order Act 1986, is also often highly relevant in the sporting arena. Furthermore, it should not be forgotten that the statutory protection which Parliament has seen fit to provide to spectators in one form or another does not affect the duty which the organisers of sporting events owe to spectators at common law.

The Safety of Sports Grounds Act 1975

The principal Act aimed at achieving a framework for the safety of those attending sports grounds is the Safety of Sports Grounds Act 1975 (as amended by the Fire Safety and Safety of Places of Sport Act 1987). This legislation, together with the subordinate legislation, are supplemented by the Home Office *Guide to Safety at Sports Grounds* (the so-called "Green Guide", already referred to). The fire certification scheme under the 1975 Act applies to any sports ground which, in the opinion of the Secretary of State, has accommodation for more than 10,000 spectators (5,000 in respect of sports grounds at which association football matches are played and which are occupied by a club which is a member of the Football League Limited or the Football Association Premier League Limited (see the Safety of Sports Grounds (Accommodation of Spectators) Order 1996 (SI 1996/499)).

A ground requiring a certificate under the Act is deemed to be a "designated sports ground", but a similar scheme applies to stands at undesignated grounds where there is covered accommodation for 500 or more spectators (see ss 26–41 of the 1987 Act). In addition, section 10 of the 1975 Act introduced a special procedure for prohibiting or restricting the admission of spectators to a sports ground, or any part of it, which involves or will involve a serious risk to them. A prohibition notice granted to a local authority under section 10 remains in force until such time as the risk is reduced to a reasonable level. Despite the safeguards in the 1975 Act, it seems that nobody perceived the appalling congestion problems which the design and layout of the Leppings Lane End of Hillsborough stadium was capable of creating.

Sporting Events (Control of Alcohol etc) Act 1985

The Sporting Events (Control of Alcohol etc) Act 1985 (as amended by s 40 of the Public Order Act 1986) was belatedly introduced following a decade-and-a-half of almost unremitting crowd violence, hooliganism and the destruction of property and transport by so-called football supporters, both in this country and abroad. The Act, which covers a broad range of mischiefs, makes it a criminal offence, *inter alia*:

(1) to cause or permit intoxicating liquor to be carried on public transport carrying passengers to and from designated sporting events, or to possess intoxicating liquor on such vehicles (s 1(2) and (3));

(2) to possess intoxicating liquor or certain articles capable of causing injury (a bottle or other container) at, or while entering, a designated sports ground during a designated sports event (s 2(1));

(3) to be drunk on a vehicle to which section 1 applies, or in a sports ground to which section 2 applies (ss 1(4) and 2(2) respectively); and

(4) to possess any article or substance whose main purpose is the emission of a flare, smoke, or visible gas (but not matches, cigarette lighters or heaters) (see s 2A, entitled "Fireworks etc.", which was introduced by Sched 1 to the Public Order Act 1986).

Where the offence alleged goes beyond simple possession of, for example, a firework, a more serious charge should be preferred. Thus, two spectators who let off a marine distress rocket at a packed Cardiff Arms Park during an international football match, killing a spectator on the opposite side of the ground, were each sentenced to three years' imprisonment, having pleaded guilty to a charge of manslaughter (see *Attorney-General's Reference (Nos 26 and 27 of 1994)* (1995) 16 Cr App R (S) 675).

The 1985 Act also regulates licensing hours for licensed premises situated within designated sports grounds (s 3), but specific provisions have subsequently been introduced to deal with private facilities for viewing sporting events (*e.g.* corporate hospitality boxes), occasional licences, clubs, and non-retail sales (see ss 5A–5D). A police constable in uniform is empowered to close a bar if it appears to him that the sale of intoxicating liquor is detrimental to the orderly conduct or safety of spectators at the event (s 6).

Bradford City – the Popplewell Report

On 11 May 1985, 38 people were killed and 400 were injured in a fire at Bradford City's Valley Parade ground. On the same day, Birmingham City and Leeds United supporters fought a pitched battle during a vital promotion match at St Andrews in Birmingham. In what proved to be one of the blackest months for English football, 38 supporters died during the European Cup Final between Liverpool and Juventus at the Heysel Stadium in Brussels on 29 May 1985 when a wall collapsed as the Italian fans attempted to escape from rampaging Liverpool "supporters". The Heysel disaster proved to be the final straw for UEFA, and English clubs were banned from taking part in European competition for five years. Popplewell J was initially appointed to conduct an inquiry into the Bradford disaster and the riot at Birmingham, and also to report on the operation of the Safety of Sports Grounds Act 1975 (Cmnd 9585). His terms of reference were later widened to include the Heysel tragedy, which appears in the final report (Cmnd 9710). The recommendations in both reports were wide ranging and provided the impetus for the Fire Safety and Safety of Places of Sport Act 1987. Referring to a long list of inquiries dating back to the Shortt Report of 1924 (in the wake of the first FA Cup Final at Wembley in 1923), and the recommendations which had been made in the intervening half century, Popplewell J said this:

> "It is to be hoped that they will be more vigorously pursued by the appropriate bodies than in the past."

How prophetic that statement proved to be in the light of subsequent events at Hillsborough. Indeed, the very first recommendation in the interim Popplewell Report was that evacuation procedures should be a matter of police training. The report also recommended that suitable and adequate exits should be provided in all sports grounds. The Working Group had even more foresight when it stressed in its recommendations on amendments to the Green Guide (recommendation 35):

> "The importance of allowing full access to the pitch where this is likely to be used as a place of safety in emergency should be plain."

The Working Group also made specific recommendations on the safe capacity of terraces and terrace packing densities (see recommendations 24–26), together with safe ingress to, and egress from, grounds. Once again, it would appear that none of those recommendations had been adequately acted upon at Hillsborough by the afternoon of 15 April 1989.

Public Order Act 1986

In the summer of 1971 a doubles match at Wimbledon involving a South African tennis player was interrupted when a number of anti-apartheid demonstrators stepped onto the court waving placards, blowing whistles and throwing leaflets. Those responsible were arrested and one was charged with using insulting behaviour likely to occasion a breach of the peace, contrary to section 5 of the Public Order Act 1936 (as amended). The justices dismissed the information without calling on the defendant to give evidence. On appeal by the prosecution the Divisional Court remitted the case to the justices to continue the hearing on the ground that insulting behaviour had been established. However, the House of Lords upheld the appeal of the defendant. The justices' decision was one of fact and could only be attacked if they had misdirected themselves in the same way that the misdirection of a jury was capable of being impugned. Their Lordships found that that had not been the case here (see *Brutus* v *Cozens* [1973] AC 854).

Putting the reasoning behind the decision in *Brutus* to one side, the case shows that spectators at sporting events will face prosecution for public order offences in appropriate circumstances. The provisions of the Public Order Act 1986 which are likely to be relevant in the context of spectator behaviour at sporting events are: section 1 (riot), section 2 (violent disorder), section 3 (affray), section 4 (causing fear or provocation of violence), section 4A (intentionally causing harassment, alarm or distress) and section 5 (causing harassment, alarm or distress). Sections 4, 4A and 5 all proscribe the use of threatening, abusive or insulting words or behaviour, or the display of any writing, sign or other visible representation which is threatening, abusive or insulting. The element of *mens rea* required for each of the offences is set out in section 6.

Part III of the Act brings together, and rationalises, the former offences relating to racial hatred and incorporates certain additional provisions. Section 17 defines "racial hatred" as hatred against a group of persons in Great Britain defined by reference to colour, race, nationality (including citizenship) or ethnic or national origins. The specific mischief of chanting racist abuse on football terraces was not covered by the Act, and that lacuna was plugged by the Football (Offences) Act 1991. Part IV of the 1986 Act, which was influenced by the findings of the Popplewell Report and had one eye on a voluntary membership scheme for football supporters, established a framework with the specific objective of quelling football hooliganism with the introduction of exclusion orders for an offence connected with football (see ss 30–37). The new measures were clearly intended to supplement the provisions of the Sporting Events (Control of Alcohol) Act 1985, although subsequent events showed that further legislation was necessary.

Fire Safety and Safety of Places of Sport Act 1987

The objective of the Fire Safety and Safety of Places of Sport Act 1987 is to provide more effective protection from the dangers caused by fire and to ensure a higher standard of safety for those attending sporting events where a serious risk to public safety might exist. The main feature of the Act, which has already been mentioned in the context of the Safety of Sports Grounds Act 1975, is the requirement to provide a fire certificate for a covered stand capable of holding 500 spectators. That statutory obligation is backed up by powers given to local authorities to take enforcement action without the need to make a preliminary application to a court.

Hillsborough – the Taylor report

Lord Justice Taylor's final report on the Hillsborough tragedy was published in January 1990 (Cmnd 962). One of the main planks of the 76 recommendations made in Part V of the report was the phased introduction of all-seater stadia for grounds designated under the Safety of Sports Grounds Act 1975. Apart from the specific findings relating to the tragedy itself, the report concluded that the facilities provided for spectators at football grounds were not merely basic, but "squalid". The denial to spectators of essential facilities at what are places of entertainment directly lowered their standard of conduct. According to the report, a basic level of safety was being ignored and higher priority needed to be given to the safety and well-being of supporters. Amongst other things, the report also recommended the improvement of perimeter fences (to be followed by their later removal), maximum capacities for enclosures and terraces, and for arrangements to be made between clubs and the police for the filling and monitoring of terraces. Indeed, effective communication, which was conspicuously absent on the fateful day at Hillsborough, is a thread which runs through the report. The co-ordination of the emergency services and specific requirements in respect of first aid, medical facilities and ambulances also feature prominently. In addition to precipitating vast improvements in the standard of football stadia in this country, the Taylor report also proved to be the catalyst for further statutory intervention by Parliament.

Football Spectators Act 1989

The laudable intention of the Football Spectators Act 1989 was to break the link between football and hooliganism. It created a Football Licensing Authority to oversee the much maligned, and ultimately ill-fated, football supporters identity-card scheme and to provide for the safety of spectators. In his final report, which was presented to Parliament only two months after the 1989 Act was introduced, Lord Justice Taylor expressed "grave doubts" about the feasibility of a national membership scheme and "serious misgivings" about its likely impact on safety, leading him to conclude that he could not lend support to the implementation of Part I of the Act. Perhaps the feature of the Act which has proved to be most useful in combatting hooliganism is the procedure for excluding offenders convicted of violence or disorder from attending matches by requiring them to attend at a police station on match days (see ss 15 and 16). On 3 June 1997, a metropolitan stipendary magistrate imposed a five-year ban on a Millwall supporter from every league ground in the country after he was found guilty of chanting racist abuse at Gillingham players during a match at Millwall's ground (*R v Ryan*, unreported).There is also power to impose restriction orders on those who commit offences outside the jurisdiction which are analogous to offences under the Act (see s 22).

Football (Offences) Act 1991

Further provision was made to deal with disorderly conduct by persons attending football matches by the Football (Offences) Act 1991 which reflects the Taylor Report's strategy against hooliganism. The Act applies to "designated" association football matches and, like the Public Order Act 1986, its provisions apply to anything done within the period beginning two hours before the advertised commencement of, and one hour after, a match (s 1 of the 1991 Act). The three activities which the Act is directed at are:

(1) the throwing of missiles at or towards the playing area, or an area adjacent thereto; and at any area in which spectators or other persons may be present. It is a defence for a person to show that he had lawful authority or excuse to do what he did (s 2);

(2) to take part in chanting of an indecent or racialist nature (s 3). Thus, football supporters who chant obscenities at players or opposing supporters will commit an offence under the 1991 Act in circumstances where the requirements of section 5 of the Public Order Act 1986 might not be satisfied; and

(3) to go onto the playing area, or an area adjacent thereto, without lawful authority or excuse (s 3).

The sanction for contravening any of those provisions is a fine not exceeding level 3 on the standard scale (which currently stands at £1,000).

Some clubs have also exercised self-help in a bid to counter hooliganism, most notably Luton Town FC which introduced a home supporters only scheme in the aftermath of a full-scale pitch battle between Luton and Millwall supporters at Luton's Kenilworth Road ground in March 1985. After initial teething problems, the scheme proved to be a success. However, the problems associated with English clubs and the national side travelling abroad still persist. Those who thought that the Heysel disaster and the subsequent lengthy ban imposed on English clubs from European competition would concentrate the minds of the thugs to mend their ways were proved wrong by the crowd trouble which led to the abandonment of the recent match between England and the Republic of Ireland in Dublin.

Even more recently, the events in Oporto, Portugal, following Manchester United's Champions' League match against FC Porto, tend to support the writer's theory that improvements in crowd behaviour in this country are due, in no small part, to more sophisticated policing techniques which have left their European counterparts lagging behind. The poor design of the Oporto ground also appears to have played a significant part in the trouble and, in that regard, we are also now arguably in a different league to most other European countries. Regrettably, the ugly scenes in Trafalgar Square following England's exit from last summer's European Football Championships show that there is a limit to which unacceptable behaviour in the name of football is capable of being resisted.

Criminal Justice and Public Order Act 1994

Ticket touts have long been the scourge of supporters, clubs and the police alike, and the seriously disruptive effect which touts can have was recognised by Lord Justice Taylor in the Hillsborough report. He identified two particular problems arising out of ticket touting at football matches, namely (1) that the presence of touts outside grounds acted as a focus for disorder since it encouraged those without tickets to travel to matches in the hope of buying tickets which sometimes led to unruly behaviour; and (2) ticket touts sold tickets on an indiscriminate basis, with the consequence that supporters of one team could find themselves among supporters of another team which foiled the best-laid plans of the police and clubs to segregate them and could lead to public disorder. The final report therefore recommended that consideration be given to the creation of an offence of selling tickets without authority (see recommendation 70). Section 166 of the Criminal Justice and Public Order Act 1994 gives statutory force to recommendation 70 by providing that:

> "(1) It is an offence for a person to sell, or offer or expose for sale, a ticket for a designated football match in any public place to which the public has access or, in the course of a trade or business, in any other place."

The present position is that in order to sell tickets for a designated football match (*i.e.* one to which s 1(1) of the Football (Offences) Act 1991 applies), the seller must have written permission from the home club, or the match organisers. Section 166 is aimed at professional touts and does not prevent a legitimate supporter from passing or selling a ticket to a friend (although doing so outside a ground on match day would fall foul of the "public place" restriction, as some have found to their cost). Section 166 also provides the police with the power to arrest without warrant and to search persons and vehicles if they reasonably suspect an offence. The penalty for contravening section 166 is a fine not exceeding level 5, which currently stands at £5,000. In due course, it may be that the provisions of section 166 will be extended by the Home Secretary to cover other sporting events for which 6,000 or more tickets are issued for sale, such as the Wimbledon tennis championships (see s 166(6)–(8)).

Other aspects of the 1994 Act which should be mentioned are the wider stop and search powers introduced by section 60, and provisions relating to aggravated trespass which potentially catch the pitch demonstrations engaged in from time to time by disenchanted supporters.

Conclusion

The legislation which has been referred to in this chapter demonstrates the will of Parliament to assist sport, and football in particular, to get its house in order. It is an example of the positive effect which central government can have when the administrators of sport do not have the will or the resources to bring about much needed changes. That intervention has clearly borne fruit in the vastly improved stadia in which football is now played in this country, and also in improved crowd behaviour. It would therefore be churlish to complain that the various statutory provisions were introduced on a piecemeal basis. The measures were undoubtedly long overdue, but without the driving force of central government behind them, the quantum leap in the level of comfort and safety which supporters enjoy at football grounds would probably never have happened. It is also self-evident that professional football owes a great debt of gratitude to Popplewell J, and especially the late Lord Taylor.

Chapter 8

Contractual Disputes

Introduction

In the context of sporting endeavour, contractual disputes frequently concern contracts of employment, and in the area of freedom of movement there has recently been significant development. The existence or otherwise of a contractual relationship between an individual or club and a governing body can have far-reaching consequences when the former wishes to challenge the disciplinary and administrative actions of the latter. Contractual wranglings occur in professional football where commitments are made, and then broken, with apparently little or no regard to the implications, typically where one or more of the parties mistakenly thinks that a verbal agreement is not binding. For example, when Osvaldo Ardiles became the manager of Tottenham Hotspur in 1993, West Bromwich Albion (WBA) threatened legal action against Tottenham for compensation, claiming that they had a "handshake deal" with Ardiles to remain as the WBA manager. Ardiles had just been paid a performance bonus for leading WBA to promotion, but no formal written contract embodying the terms of his engagement with the club had ever been drawn up. The recent transfer "bung" scandal involving the former Arsenal (now Leeds United) manager, George Graham, reveals a murkier side of football in which formal contracts capable of being subjected to scrutiny have no place. In that twilight world, the parties involved implicitly rely on one another to honour commitments which are in clear contravention of FA regulations. The above examples underline the fact that contractual arrangements in the world of sport often provide fertile ground for dispute.

Freedom of contract and movement

It is now well-established law that the terms of an agreement between employers which seek to regulate labour and to impose mutual restrictions on the re-employment of former employees are liable to be struck out as being contrary to the public interest, or on the ground that they effectively amount to an employer–employee covenant (see *Esso Petroleum Co Ltd* v *Harper's Garage (Stourport) Ltd* [1968] AC 269).

Eastham v Newcastle United FC – breaking the "retain and transfer" system

Freedom of contract in professional football in this country emerged following the case of *Eastham* v *Newcastle United Football Club Ltd* [1964] Ch 413. In accordance with the rules of the FA, the defendant club operated a "retain and transfer" system which meant that a player could be retained by the club after the termination of his contract of employment, thereby preventing him from playing for another club. There was no obligation on the part of the defendant club to re-employ a player, and he could also be placed on the transfer list. Unless another club was prepared to pay the stipulated transfer fee, the player could not obtain employment elsewhere. The plaintiff claimed that those conditions were in unreasonable restraint of trade and were not binding on him. The club argued that the conditions were necessary in the interest of the proper and stable organisation of the game.

Wilberforce J (as he then was) accepted that the club's interest was legitimate, but was not satisfied that the system it operated imposed no greater restraint on the plaintiff's freedom of employment than was necessary to protect that interest. Although the rules were an agreement between employers only, they were designed to affect their employees' freedom of employment and could therefore be challenged on the same ground as if they had been incorporated into an agreement between employer and employee. A declaration was therefore made that the system was invalid, both in respect of the defendant club and the rules of the FA which enabled them to be operated. The decision in *Eastham* dismantled a restrictive practice which had been exploited by clubs since 1912 when the Aston Villa player, Harry Kingaby, failed at the first hurdle in an attempt to challenge his club's right to demand a transfer fee as a condition of releasing him from his contract (see *Kingaby* v *Aston Villa* (1913) *The Times*, 28 March (reference to the case can be found in the judgment of Wilberforce J in *Eastham*).

Restraint of trade post-Eastham

A similar outcome to that in *Eastham* was achieved in *Greig* v *Insole* [1978] 1 WLR 302 where a resolution of the International Cricket

Conference disqualifying any player from playing in Test matches who had taken part in a match arranged by the Australian entrepreneur, Kerry Packer, and a resolution of the English Test and County Cricket Board (TCCB) to like effect, were held to be void as being in unreasonable restraint of trade. In contrast, when Graham Gooch led a cricketing tour to South Africa in 1984 in breach of the sporting boycott imposed on that country at the time, he and his fellow "rebels" did not mount a legal challenge against their subsequent ban from Test match cricket by the TCCB. In the same year in which he was seriously injured fighting Chris Eubank, Michael Watson sued his manager, Mickey Duff, claiming that the standard form of boxer–manager promotional agreement for professional boxing was in restraint of trade. Scott J agreed, finding that the contract, which had been drafted by the sport's governing body, the Boxing Board of Control, permitted a conflict of interest to occur where the manager also acted as the boxer's promoter. It was also held (*per curiam*) that where a case involved an attack on the agreement, the Board could not be impartial for the purposes of section 24(1) of the Arbitration Act 1950 (which empowers a court to revoke the authority of an arbitrator) since it had a significant interest in the issues raised in such an action (see *Watson* v *Prager* [1991] 3 All ER 487).

Interlocutory relief – is a contractual relationship necessary?

A restraint of trade argument proved to be the basis of a successful challenge by three Welsh football clubs against a resolution of the Welsh Football Association that they could not play on their home grounds when they took part in English domestic league competitions below Premier and Endsleigh League levels (see *Newport Association Football Club Ltd and others* v *Football Association of Wales Ltd* [1995] 2 All ER 87). As a consequence of the resolution, the plaintiffs claimed that their revenue from home gates and sponsorship had dramatically decreased, and sought (1) a declaration that the defendant's resolution was in unreasonable restraint of trade, and (2) an injunction restraining the defendant from acting in restraint of trade. Jacob J granted the plaintiffs interlocutory relief, despite the fact that no contractual relationship existed between the plaintiffs and the defendant. Where a contract or other arrangement is found to be in unreasonable restraint of trade, it is void and unenforceable, but Jacob J appears to have treated a claim for a declaration as a cause of action in itself, following *dicta* of Wilberforce J in *Eastham* (see p 92h-j of Jacob J's judgment, referring to p 440 of the report in *Eastham*). In other words, even if there is no cause of action in the conventional sense, a party to a contract is still entitled to ask a court to declare that the contract is null and void. However, the granting of an injunction in the absence of a contractual nexus between the parties is difficult to reconcile with the steadfast refusal of the Divisional Court to grant leave for judicial review of sport's governing bodies, as Chapter 9 shows.

The injunction which was recently obtained by the Welsh rugby union player, Mark Jones, allowing him to play rugby pending an appeal against a ban, is tantamount to a finding that to prevent him from doing so would constitute an unreasonable restraint of trade, having regard to the circumstances in which the ban was imposed. On the other hand, if a disciplinary hearing observes the rules of natural justice, and a ban is imposed which is commensurate with the offence, it is extremely difficult to see how such an outcome could be challenged on the ground of restraint of trade, or any other ground for that matter. Another interesting point to note from the case is the judge's finding that a form of contract existed between the parties by virtue of the player's registration with the Welsh Rugby Football Union and his agreement to be subjected to its disciplinary procedure (see *Jones and another* v *Welsh Rugby Football Union* (1997) *The Times*, 6 March). It is debatable whether the application would have succeeded had it not been for that finding. If the decision of Jacob J to grant an injunction to the plaintiff clubs in the *Newport* case was correct, then the absence of a contractual relationship should not matter. However, if all an applicant for judicial review had to do was bring a private law action instead of seeking a public law remedy under Rules of the Supreme Court Ord 53, there would surely have been a flood of writs a long time ago against sport's governing bodies.

It would be surprising if the *Newport* case could not have been founded on a contract of some kind. It will be a rare case where an exchange of mutual rights and obligations cannot be found. The most obvious consideration which passes from clubs is the annual affiliation fees paid to their governing bodies, invariably to meet administrative costs. Even if a financial payment is missing, clubs and players agree, expressly or impliedly, to abide by the rules and regulations of their governing body, and to accept any reasonable disciplinary sanctions that may be imposed. In return, each club has the benefit of being part of a network of clubs which is also affiliated to the governing body and which has similarly agreed to be bound by the rights and obligations of being a member of the network. The governing body over-arches the network by organising and administering competition between clubs, by impliedly agreeing to treat each of its members fairly and with impartiality, and to mediate in disputes between its members. Ultimately, the effectiveness of disciplinary sanctions must hinge on a contractual obligation on the part of clubs and players to be bound by them, otherwise, a club could simply ignore any penalty its governing body might care to impose. If there was *no* contract in the *Newport* case, what power did the Welsh FA have to impose sanctions on the plaintiffs? If no such power existed, there would appear to have been no need for injunctive relief.

The *Bosman* ruling

The freedom of contract and movement of professional sportsmen within EC Member States has recently been the subject of what is widely regarded as a landmark ruling by the European Court of Justice (*Union Royale Belge des Sociétés de Football Association ASBL v Bosman* (1996) All ER (EC) 97). Jean-Marc Bosman was an unremarkable player employed on a salary of approximately £2,000 per month by the Belgian club Standard Liège. At the end of his contract he was offered a new, one-year deal at half his existing salary. The proposal was the minimum wage permitted by the Belgian FA. When he refused to accept the offer, Bosman was placed on the transfer list. The amount of the compulsory transfer fee was fixed at approximately £300,000 which represented five times the amount his club had paid for him. When no Belgian side expressed an interest in him, Bosman contacted a French club (US Dunkerque) and agreement was reached between them over his salary. The two clubs agreed a fee for the player's temporary transfer and all that was required was a transfer certificate from the Belgian FA in order to sanction the agreement. However, Liège had doubts over Dunkerque's ability to pay the transfer fee and did not apply for the certificate. Consequently, the deal fell through and Bosman was suspended by Liège.

Bosman sued Liège in the Belgian courts claiming damages for breach of contract and challenged the legality of the transfer system. The Belgian appeal court referred the case to the European Court of Justice (ECJ) for a preliminary ruling on the following issues of European law:

(1) whether the transfer system infringed Article 48 of the EC Treaty which enshrines the right of workers to free movement within Member States;

(2) whether Article 85 of the Treaty was being infringed in that competition was being distorted by the transfer system; and

(3) whether there was a violation of Article 86 of the EC Treaty in that there was an abuse of a dominant position which affected trade between Member States.

The Belgian national court referred two questions to the ECJ, namely:

(1) whether Articles 48, 85 and 86 of the EC Treaty prohibited a football club from requiring and receiving the payment of a sum of money upon the engagement by a new employing club of one of its players who has come to the end of his contract; and

(2) whether the aforementioned articles prohibited the national and international sporting associations or federations from including in their respective regulations provisions restricting access of foreign players from the European Union to the competitions they organise.

The Advocate-General recommended that the two questions be answered affirmatively, and cited two previous sporting cases which the ECJ had been asked to rule on, namely *Walrave v Union Cycliste International* [1974] ECR 1407 and *Dona v Mantero* [1976] ECR 1333. The ECJ upheld the recommendation and ruled as follows:

(1) Article 48 precluded the application of rules laid down by sporting associations, under which a professional footballer who was a national of one Member State could not, on the expiry of his contract with a club, be employed by a club of another Member State unless the latter club had paid to the former club a transfer, training or development fee.

(2) Article 48 precluded the application of rules laid down by sporting associations under which, in matches in competitions they organised, football clubs could field only a limited number of professional players who were nationals of other Member States.

(3) The direct effect of Article 48 could not be relied on in support of claims relating to a fee in respect of transfer, training or development which had already been paid on, or was still payable under an obligation which arose before

the date of the judgment, except by those who had brought court proceedings or raised an equivalent claim under the applicable national law before that date.

The implications of *Bosman*

The long-term implications of the *Bosman* ruling are still unclear, and opinions are mixed as to its significance for football in particular, and sport in general. It is clear that the decision only affects players who have come to the end of their contracts and who will now be able to offer their services freely in the "shop window". When his contract comes to an end, a player can now negotiate directly with a club and bypass the transfer tribunal. In short, professional footballers will now share the same rights as any other employee who provides a service. The most obvious short-term effect of the ruling has been an influx of foreign stars enticed to this country by the lifting of the "three foreign players per side" restriction, and huge salaries funded by stratospheric payments for television rights. The new culture created by *Bosman* appears to have been adopted by the top English football clubs with little fuss. This is probably due to the fact that, unlike other EC Member States, freedom of contract in football has been firmly established in this country since the *Eastham* case.

Nevertheless, top sides like Manchester United wasted no time renegotiating their players' contracts (particularly the young stars) which will tie them to the club for a much longer period than had hitherto been the case. However, promising young players in the lower divisions will be far less willing to sign long-term contracts for obvious reasons. Smaller clubs will also be cautious about entering into lengthy financial commitments when form, fitness and fortunes can change so quickly. Indeed, the implications for the smaller clubs could be serious. Historically, they have been forced to sell their best players to ensure their survival, and transfer fees meant that money was kept in the game. In the post-*Bosman* environment, the distribution of wealth generated by transfers may well shift discernibly from clubs to players. Historically, players who gave loyal service to one club were allowed a free transfer at the end of their career which enabled them to secure a better short-term pay deal from their new club. Now, players can enjoy the same benefit throughout their careers, and loyalty to one club is not in their best financial interests – quite the reverse.

Perhaps the most significant aspect of *Bosman* was the finding that the rules by which football governed itself were unlawful. It concerns the fundamental question of where the limits of the powers of sport's governing bodies lie. One senses that everyone is looking over their shoulders to see where the next legal challenge is going to come from and that sport has reached a critical point in its evolution. The recent failure by Middlesbrough FC to reverse a three-point deduction and £50,000 fine for failing to fulfil a Premier League fixture left most interested observers speculating whether the club would pursue the matter further through the courts. The FA Commission which heard the appeal was faced with two dilemmas. First, as Dan Tench noted in his article in the *Independent* on 26 March 1997, there is an apparent conflict between rule 19 of the Premier League's Rules and rule 7 of its Power of Commission (agreed to by all the member clubs when the Premier League was incepted). Under rule 19 the only sanction imposed on a club which fails to fulfil its fixtures is to pay compensation to the opposing club. However, under rule 7 of the Power of Commission the League can "impose such penalties by way of reprimand, fine, suspension, deduction of points, expulsion", or any combination of those punishments as it thinks fit. Secondly, the other clubs who were locked in a relegation battle with Middlesbrough had made veiled threats of legal action if the three points *were* restored. At the time of writing (before the end of the 1996/97 football season) no action has yet been taken.

Freedom of movement within the United Kingdom post-Bosman

A particularly pertinent question arising out of the Bosman ruling which has yet to be ruled upon by the courts (either national or European), is whether players who move between clubs within the United Kingdom have an unfettered right to do so when their contracts expire. The fact that there are four independent associations governing football within the United Kingdom ought to be irrelevant since the four countries who make up the Union (*i.e.* England, Wales, Scotland and Northern Ireland) are not individual EC member states. Moreover, it would be perverse if a player was entitled to move freely between member states, but could not do so if he desired a transfer between clubs within a particular member state. In this country, such a situation would fly in the face of the decision in *Eastham* and introduce by the back door a restrictive practice which was firmly dismissed by Wilberforce J over thirty years ago.

Transfer deadlines

The setting of arbitrary transfer deadlines and excluding players from playing in a cup competition after they have played for another club in the same competition in the same season (colloquially referred to as "cup tied") are two further associated practices which arguably constitute an unlawful restraint of trade and a restriction on the movement of employee-players. The mischief which transfer deadlines are aimed at is clubs obtaining an unfair advantage over others by acquiring players beyond a certain date in order, for example, to enhance a cup run or challenge for a league title. A court of first instance in Belgium has asked the European Court of Justice for a preliminary ruling on such a question, namely whether the rules of a sports federation, which prohibit a club from fielding a player in a competition for the first time if he has been engaged after a specified date, are contrary to the EC Treaty in the case of a professional player who is a national of a member state, notwithstanding the sporting reasons advanced by the federations concerned for justifying the rules, *i.e.* the desire to prevent clubs from distorting competitions (see *Jyri Lehtonen and ASBL Castors Canada Dry Namur-Braine* v *ASBL Fédération Royale Belge des Sociétés de Basketball*, Case C-176/96, ref: 96/C197/32). A ruling against the setting of transfer deadlines would have a significant impact on a large number of sports which adopt such restrictive practices, particularly football. If they are held to be illegal, and there is a good chance that they will, it must surely follow that the practice of cup-tying players is similarly unsustainable.

The activity of the Belgian courts in this particular area of sports-related litigation is further evidenced by the case of *Christelle Deliege* v *ASBL Ligue Francophone de Judo et Disciplines Associées and ABSL Ligue Belge de Judo*, Case C-51/96, ref: 96/C133/25. There, the Belgian court has asked whether or not rules which require a professional or semi-professional sportsman to have been authorised or selected by his national federation in order to enable him to compete in European competition, are contrary to the EC Treaty and, in particular, Articles 59 to 66, and Articles 85 and 86. At the time of writing, a ruling has yet to be made.

Performance-related clauses

It is an invariable feature of the inflated transfers paid for professional footballers that the transfer contract will provide for increments to be paid in the event that a player plays a certain number of games or scores a certain number of goals, for his new club and/or his country. In *Bournemouth and Boscombe Athletic Football Club Co Ltd* v *Manchester United Football Club Ltd* (1980) *The Times*, 21 May Bournemouth FC claimed that a former player, Ted MacDougall, whom the club had transferred to Manchester United in 1972, was not given a reasonable opportunity to play for his new club and so was unable to score a specified number of goals which would have entitled Bournemouth to an uplift in the transfer fee agreed between the two clubs. The contract did not give the player an express right to be included in the Manchester United side.

The Court of Appeal held (by a majority) that it was an implied term of the transfer agreement that the player would be given a reasonable opportunity to score the requisite goals. According to Lord Denning and Donaldson LJ such a term was required in order to give the contract business efficacy. An appropriately worded clause should therefore be inserted in such a contract and, it would seem, it is not necessary to show bad faith on the part of the defendant club. However, the dissenting judgment of Brightman LJ seems better to reflect the reality of the situation. Manchester United had changed its manager following MacDougall's transfer, and the new manager, Tommy Docherty, simply did not rate him. That judgment was made in good faith, and to compel a manager to pick an unsatisfactory player would interfere with his discretion to field what he considers to be the best side. He would get little thanks or understanding from his side's supporters for fielding a team of mediocre players for no other reason than that he was obliged to give them all a reasonable number of games.

Material considerations in such a case would include: how was the player performing; was he injured; and what sort of relationship did he enjoy with his fellow players and manager?. In a case where the contract provides for the payment of a specific sum in respect of each game played or goal scored, the loss would not be susceptible to precise quantification, and the aggrieved club would therefore have to claim general damages. There was no suggestion in the *Bournemouth* case that the player's disciplinary record excluded him from selection but, if that had been the case, it may well have provided Manchester United with a strong defence. By definition, a player cannot be selected if he is subject to a ban imposed by his sport's governing body. Internal breaches of club discipline might also provide a valid line of defence in such cases. One of the scenarios in Chapter 12 gives examples of pleadings in a case such as this albeit with somewhat irreverent allegations!

Agreements conferring exclusive jurisdiction

In the lead-up to the 1996 Olympic Games in Atlanta, the Juridicial Commission of the International Olympic Committee, with the assistance of a number of advisors, drafted an entry form which, it was proposed, would be signed by all the competitors who intended to participate in the games as a condition of their entry. One term of entry provided that any dispute which might arise during the course of the Games would be submitted exclusively to the Court of Arbitration for Sport (CAS) which, for the first time, was to have an *ad hoc* division of arbitrators in Atlanta to enable cases to be heard swiftly. The relevant section of the entry form concluded as follows:

> "I shall not institute any claim, arbitration or litigation, or seek any other form of relief in any other court or tribunal."

At the time, a certain amount of disquiet was expressed about competitors being required to forego their legal rights to pursue a claim in the traditional way (*i.e.* through the courts) in the event that they were aggrieved by a ruling against them. The motivation behind the terms of the entry form, and the establishment of an *ad hoc* division of the CAS was apparently to supplement the athletes' rights, not to deprive them of their rights of redress. However, in drafting the terms, the International Olympic Committee (IOC) cannot have ignored the protracted (and highly public) cases involving Diane Modhal, Katrin Krabbe and Butch Reynolds, and the massive damages award which was made to the latter following a successful challenge through the courts to a four-year ban for alleged drug abuse. All the British competitors at the Games signed the form and, as far as the writer is aware, none of the competitors challenged its validity. The chance of competing in an Olympic Games may be a strong incentive for agreeing to forego certain legal rights but, ultimately, the competitors were free to choose whether or not to sign the entry form. Therefore, a plea of *non est factum* would almost certainly fail if a competitor who signed the form subsequently sought to impugn the conditions of entry.

The arbitrators heard, and determined, five challenges during the course of the Games, all of which were described as "athlete friendly" by Michael Beloff QC, the member on the panel from Britain. Since the Olympic Charter is underpinned by principles of fair play, and the arbitration panel in Atlanta consisted of many emminent lawyers and judges, it is hardly surprising that the rules of natural justice and due process were adhered to. Furthermore, the fact that no one appears to have challenged the validity of the "exclusion clause" (for want of a better expression) in the courts suggests that the competitors were content with the improved machinery for hearing disputes. It seems reasonable to conclude, therefore, that the reservations expressed about the conditions of entry were misplaced, and that the IOC could have provided a lead for other major sporting competitions to follow. The residual concern, however, must be that not all the sporting bodies which are attracted to the idea of excluding traditional rights of redress will have adequate machinery to dispose satisfactorily of disputes internally.

Inducing breach of contract

The somewhat unorthodox and informal practices referred to in the introduction to the chapter extend, from time to time, to allegations of "poaching" players and managers. Leicester City FC lost two managers in quick succession – Brian Little to Aston Villa, followed by Mark McGhee to Wolverhampton Wanderers – in extremely acrimonious circumstances. In 1994 Everton FC was fined £75,000 and ordered to pay £50,000 compensation to Norwich City by the Premier League after Everton was found guilty of enticing the Norwich manager, Mike Walker, to leave his club. The inquiry found that Everton had "indirectly induced" Walker to leave Norwich by fuelling speculation in the media, whether intentionally or otherwise. Rumours of managerial musical chairs and dissatisfied players are the stock-in trade of the popular press, which is ably assisted by unscrupulous clubs, players and agents. Those involved in such practices are either ignorant of, or choose to ignore, the law relating to interference with the performance of a contract, interference with a contractual relationship, and interference with trade. It is a tort for a third party knowingly to induce a party to a contract to breach the contract without lawful justification (see *Lumley* v *Gye* [1853] 2 E&B 216). Additionally, unlawful threats by contracting parties to breach their contracts may constitute the tort of intimidation (see *Rookes* v *Barnard* [1964] AC 1129). Temperamental players should beware!

Infringement of copyright and trade marks

Sport is big business, and vast profits are made from the merchandising of famous sportsmen, clubs, brand names etc. The contracts of a player will invariably contain an express provision governing the rights to name and character merchandising. This may grant the club or sporting body exclusive rights to exploit the player's name and image subject to a royalty based on sales, or a flat fee. Top players, whose earnings potentials seem to be virtually limitless nowadays, will almost certainly retain the right to enter into lucrative contracts with clothing, footwear and other sponsors. For example, Eric Cantona has applied to register his famous number 7, used in conjunction with his name as a trademark under The Trade Marks Act 1994. If a player's name or image is used without any contractual right or other permission, the immediate remedy is a prohibitory injunction restraining any further sales. The accompanying writ should also seek an order for the delivery-up of any remaining stock, together with a request for an account to be taken, payment to the aggrieved party of the amount found to be due on the account, and damages. In such cases, the relevant trading standards authority should be notified, and a criminal prosecution may also follow, probably under the Trades Descriptions Act 1968.

It is beyond the scope of this book to explain how the law of copyright protects trade marks, names etc. Suffice it to say that the exploitation of brand names and logos extends to the Olympic symbol, and legislation has therefore been passed to protect the Olympic symbol from unauthorised commercial exploitation. The Olympic Symbol etc (Protection) Act 1995, which came into force on 20 September 1995, creates a quasi-property right to the use of the Olympic symbol and certain words associated with the Olympic Games. Before the Act was introduced, no "property" rights attached to the symbol. The British Olympic Association (BOA), as the body designated to be the proprietor of the right by the Secretary of State, has the exclusive right to exploit the symbol, but not otherwise to dispose of it. Civil remedies are provided for any infringement of the BOA's right under sections 6 and 7 of the Act. There is also a criminal sanction for unauthorised use of the symbol or associated words (under s 8), but it is a defence if the defendant can show that he believed on reasonable grounds that what he did was not an infringement.

Chapter 9

Medicine and Drugs in Sport

Introduction

Medical and drug issues both have a significant impact on sport, the latter having had a seriously detrimental effect on sport's image and credibility. In certain respects the two issues require separate consideration, although medicine is a powerful tool in the fight against drug abuse in sport (see below). Contrary to the common perception that boxing is the most dangerous sport, that title goes to horse-riding (in terms of fatalities) and rugby claims first prize for the number of serious injuries sustained per participant. Even angling is not safe. The Royal Society for the Prevention of Accidents recorded 262 deaths in the course of angling between 1986 and 1991. Those statistics, however, have not prevented three attempts being made in Parliament to ban boxing over the past 30 years.

Are the physical benefits of sport overstated? There is no evidence to show that sport increases life-expectancy and, in fact, it is the single largest killer for those over 40 years old, with squash and long-distance running being particular "at risk" activities. The importance of medicine in sport has been reflected in the establishment of a number of specialist bodies including the National Sports Medicine Institute and the British Association of Sport and Medicine. The Royal Society of Medicine set up a specialist sports section in 1994 and the Football Association runs the National Rehabilitation and Sports Injuries Centre at Lilleshall.

Medicine can influence the rule-makers to change the laws of a game. For example, concerns expressed about serious neck injuries caused by collapsed scrums in rugby matches led to the introduction of a new, phased sequence of engagement in colts matches in 1991 (see the discussion of *Smoldon* in Chapter 5), and the power to award penalties where a referee concludes that one pack is deliberately taking a scrum down. Medical evidence can also play an instrumental part in the forensic process of establishing whether an injury was inflicted intentionally or otherwise, tell-tale stud or teeth marks being obvious signs of foul play. Invariably, the level of medical facilities will depend on the level at which any given sport is played and the resources available, both financially and in terms of manpower. Players are, of course, the stock-in-trade of professional clubs, which therefore have a vested interest in down-playing the significance of any injury. A failure to disclose the fact that a player has a serious injury may be an actionable misrepresentation by omission, but the risk of that happening is probably more apparent than real since a purchasing club nearly always takes the precaution of carrying out a medical examination on a player it is proposing to buy. Such an examination will almost certainly be a condition of insurance cover imposed by a club's insurers. A purchasing club may also protect itself by inserting a clause in a player's contract entitling the club to rescind his contract of employment in the event that a player is forced to retire due to a pre-existing injury. Such an arrangement apparently existed between West Ham United FC and the Portugese player, Paolo Futre, who was forced to retire from the game after playing only a handful of games for the club.

The arguments surrounding boxing persist and, not surprisingly, go to the top of the agenda every time a fatality or serious injury occurs. The British Medical Association is in the vanguard of the anti-boxing lobby, but the medical profession continues to assist in ensuring that boxing is as safe as possible. Following the serious brain damage suffered by the boxer Michael Watson in the final round of his world title fight against Chris Eubank in 1991, the British Boxing Board of Control introduced new safeguards to ensure that injured boxers received immediate ringside treatment and swift transfer to hospital. The consensus of boxing commentators is that the improvements which were introduced may well have saved the life of Gerald McLellan who suffered a blood clot in his brain during his WBC title fight with Nigel Benn at the London Arena on 25 February 1995.

Medical matters

Sporting injuries occur in a variety of ways and, ignoring those caused by crowd violence etc, there are five distinct causal factors:

(1) physical contact, whether lawful or unlawful;
(2) incorrect training, coaching or instruction;
(3) incorrect or faulty equipment;
(4) the condition of the playing surface;
(5) drugs and inappropriate medical advice, treatment and medication.

The significance of effective medical advice, facilities and treatment in combatting sports-related injuries is underlined by a study of a Scottish Premier League club's (Heart of Midlothian) players undertaken over a three-year period between 1990 and 1993. The study revealed that of a total of 27 players, 94 significant injuries were sustained, 79% of which were sustained in matches (the remaining 21% in training). The average time "out of action" was 13 weeks, giving a massive total of 364 weeks for the entire squad with a corresponding loss of productivity to the club. Midfield players were found to suffer the most injuries (39%), with the most common anatomical injury being to the thigh, followed by the knee. Not surprisingly, the most common soft tissue injuries were muscle and ligament problems. Skeletal injuries accounted for 6% of the total. Players over the age of 26 appeared to be more prone to injuries, although no correlation could be drawn between the number of games played and any increased likelihood of injuries (see McGregor and Rae, "The Review of Injuries to Professional Footballers in Premier Football Teams (1990/92)" *Scottish Medical Journal* 40:016-018).

An article which appeared in *The Lancet* on 10 June 1995, entitled "Epidemiology of Rugby Football Injuries" by Garraway and MacLeod, confirmed the enormous waste of resources caused by sporting injuries, when it concluded that 28% of injury episodes to rugby players resulted in absence from employment, or school/college work, for an average of 18 days. Placing those localised studies into a wider context, it has been estimated that approximately 19 million sports injuries occur in England and Wales each year, costing some £500 million in treatment and absence from work. The price placed on the physical damage to participants is put at £240 million. The article by Garraway and MacLeod concluded that:

> "Rugby injuries are an important source of morbidity in young men. They need to be better understood if their frequency and consequences are to be reduced."

The absence of any statutory or other requirement to maintain records of injuries in most sports makes it unlikely that such an advance in knowledge will occur, or at least not at any kind of appreciable rate. Until that happens the vast majority of professional football and rugby clubs will remain ignorant of the precise cost to them of having players sidelined through injury. However, even if they were aware of the facts, what action could clubs and managers take to reduce the crippling expense of injury? Adequate insurance cover is an obvious precaution, together with an appreciation that a significant financial investment needs to be made if sports injuries are to be kept at the lowest possible level. Rule changes also have a contribution to make in reducing the risk of on-pitch injuries, and the phased sequence of engagement of rugby scrums has already been identified as one such measure. The World Cup Finals in 1994 was perhaps not the best place to test for the first time FIFA's directive to referees to punish the tackle from behind, but the rule change has now been integrated and accepted as part of the regulatory framework of the game and, whilst the cynical challenge has not been eradicated altogether, players who commit it can be under no illusions as to the sanctions they will face. The choice of sport clearly has a bearing on the likelihood of injury, with so-called "high intensity" sports such as boxing, rugby and ice hockey carrying a greater risk than "low intensity" activities, including bowling, golf and snooker. It is interesting to note that whilst the "high intensity" category is dominated by physical contact sports, it also includes sprinting, which involves short, concerted bursts of effort, thereby increasing the risk of injury (for tables showing the various categories, see McGregor FRCS, "Sport and Injuries – Is There a Price to Pay?" (1996) *Sport and the Law Journal* 37).

Hitherto, the discussion has concentrated exclusively on participants, but the tragedies referred to in Chapter 7 underline the importance of providing adequate medical facilities for spectators. Indeed, arguably it demands a higher priority given the potential for large-scale injury whenever a large crowd gathers. By all accounts, the arrangements at Hillsborough were lamentable. Dr John Ashton, a senior lecturer at Liverpool University who was inside the ground, is quoted as saying: "at 3.30 pm there were no medical staff apart from one or two St John Ambulencemen. There was no equipment and only one ambulance". Access problems to the pitch meant that vital resuscitation equipment did not arrive until about 4.15 pm, too late for many of the casualties. Newly built or modified stadia such as Twickenham and Middlesbrough FC's Riverside Stadium have incorporated access ways for vehicles in the event of an emergency, but most grounds remain fully enclosed despite other improvements. Historically, football clubs have relied on voluntary first-aid personnel, although the presence of trained paramedics at grounds is becoming more widespread. The absence of any statutory requirement to provide such facilities inevitably means that their presence will be dictated by financial resources, but in the light of earlier events there is a strong argument that a common law duty exists on the part of organisers to ensure that adequate medical facilities are provided. The reader is referred to Chapter 5 for a discussion of the general duty of organisers and the circumstances in which they have been found liable to spectators.

Medical negligence

The self-inflicted injury which Paul Gascoigne suffered in a reckless tackle on Gary Charles during the 1991 FA Cup Final nearly ended a brilliant career (the fact that it could just as easily have finished Charles' career is often overlooked). Gascoigne's future in football was saved by the surgical team which replaced his torn cruciate knee ligament with an artificial one. Whether Gascoigne has ever scaled the great heights he achieved at the 1990 World Cup Finals is debatable, but it is beyond doubt that his highly lucrative playing days would have been prematurely cut short without medical intervention. It is extremely doubtful whether he would have recovered from such an injury had he sustained it a mere 20 years ago, such have been the advances made in the treatment of knee injuries.

Gascoigne's experience demonstrates the importance of medicine in sport, but whilst careers are often saved by surgery some are interrupted or even blighted by negligent treatment or advice. The Spanish golfer, Jose-Maria Olazabal, whose prematurely arthritic feet threatened to cut short his career, is said to have been urged by lawyers to sue the US clinic where he initially attended for treatment following his enforced withdrawal from the European Ryder Cup team in September 1995. The alleged diagnosis made by the clinic – rheumatoid arthritis of the feet – led to a course of treatment which did not provide Olazabal with sufficient relief to enable him to play in any tournaments during 1996. It was only when he attended a clinic in Munich in November 1996 that he began to make a recovery. The German doctor he consulted diagnosed a hernia at the base of Olazabal's spine as the cause of his pain and appropriate treatment enabled him to make a winning return to the European tour in February 1997. Despite the fact that Olazabal can still only play two weeks in succession, and will miss tournaments during the year, he has declined to take action against the US clinic. Not as reticent, the athlete Liz McColgan has threatened legal action against the doctors who advised and then performed what she claimed was needless surgery.

The point has already been made that in the context of medical treatment, the degree of skill and knowledge of the defendant are taken into account when determining the standard of care in a particular case (see *Bolam* v *Friern Hospital Management Committee* [1957] 1 WLR 582). The standard is that of "the ordinary skilled man exercising and professing to have that special skill" (per McNair J in *Bolam* at p 586). Once the level of skill contended for by the defendant has been established, the test is an objective one and is encapsulated in the words of Lord President Clyde in *Hunter* v *Hanley* [1955] SLT 213 at 217:

> "In the realm of diagnosis and treatment there is ample scope for genuine difference of opinion and one man clearly is not negligent merely because his conclusion differs from that of other professional men, nor because he has displayed less skill or knowledge than others would have shown. The true test ... is whether he has been proved to be guilty of such failure as no doctor of ordinary skill would be guilty of if acting with ordinary care."

Accordingly, if a defendant acts in accordance with a practice which is accepted at the time as appropriate by a responsible body of professional medical opinion skilled in the particular form of treatment (which might be as small as 10%), he will not be negligent even if there is an equally competent body of opinion in favour of a different technique. Public policy considerations and, in particular, the wish to avoid the practice of defensive medicine which is threatening to emasculate medical practice in the United States, have militated against the courts being quick to make findings of liability against doctors and surgeons in this country (see *e.g. Roe* v *Minister of Health* [1954] 2 QB 66).

Perhaps the first question which a seriously injured player will ask a doctor or surgeon is: "will I ever play again?". In the absence of an express and unequivocal promise to that effect (or any other promise for that matter), a court would be reluctant to find that an implied undertaking had been given (see *Thake* v *Maurice* [1986] QB 644). In any case, except for the most straightforward of surgical procedures, it is most unlikely that a doctor or surgeon would give anything approximating a definitive promise that a particular outcome will be achieved. Perhaps Olazabal had those considerations in mind when he took the view that the delay in overcoming his injury was simply the rub of the green.

Managers and coaches

Anecdotal evidence also suggests that managers often ignore medical advice and take calculated risks in fielding players who are carrying injuries, but, so far as the writer is aware, no legal action has ever been brought against a manager or club for aggravating an injury by encouraging someone to play when they should not. In Italy, an unsuccessful manslaughter charge was brought against the manager of the Italian Boxer, Angelo Jacopucci, who slipped into a coma and subsequently died following a fight with the British middleweight, Alan Minter, in 1978. The prosecution case against both the manager and referee was that they should have stopped the fight before the final round. The ringside doctor was convicted of a similar charge for failing to take adequate medical action after Jacopucci was knocked down. He received a suspended sentence and was ordered to pay compensation to Jacopucci's widow. Those proceedings took place in Bologna, where manslaughter charges arising out of the death of Ayrton Senna at Imola in 1994 are currently being heard against Frank Williams and other members of the Williams Formula 1 racing team. However, there the comparison ends as the prosecution case against Williams' management concerns alleged defective design and construction faults in Senna's car, as opposed to a failure to prevent him from suffering further, unnecessary punishment, or a medical misjudgment. Finally, it also seems reasonable to assume that injuries are caused or aggravated by participants themselves. The pressure of retaining a place in a team, and the desire to maximise an invariably short career, means that players often train and compete whilst carrying injuries, either with or without the knowledge of coaches and managers. An element of collusion between player and coach/manager may often take place. In an appropriate case there is no reason why legal liability should not attach to a coach or manager who engages in such practices, *a fortiori* if the coach selects a player in the face of medical advice that the player should not be playing due to injury. Any complicity on the part of the player may result in a finding of contributory negligence.

The scourge of drugs

> "Cheating in sport, I fear, is particularly a reflection of today's society. Drugs and the unprincipled pursuit of wealth and fame at any cost now threaten our very social fabric." (per the Honourable Charles Dubin CJ, *Dubin Inquiry into Drugs and Banned Practices in Sport*)

Drugs can enhance performance but they can also kill – a fatal risk that the cheats in sport either ignore or choose to take in return for what they believe will be short-term glory. The perennial problem confronting sport's governing bodies has been to stay ahead of the drugs cheats. There is ample evidence to show that weightlifters and athletes who participate in field events regularly abuse anabolic steroids and other performance-enhancing drugs. The aim has been to develop effective methods of drug detection and to maintain a list of banned substances. Administrators also face the almost constant dilemma of having to distinguish between those who take lawfully prescribed drugs for a medical condition, but which contain banned substances, and those who are out-and-out cheats. In this country the body responsible for dope-testing is the Sports Council, which runs an IOC accredited laboratory in London. For a number of years the Sports Council has published "white" and "black" drug lists and, in conjunction with the British Olympic Association (BOA), produces a booklet entitled *Drugs and Sport*, which claims to provide a comprehensive guide to the responsible use of drugs in sport. Samples are submitted for testing, and the results are then provided to the appropriate governing body to enable further investigation or action to be taken. When an Olympic Games takes place, all the British participants and their respective governing bodies are subject to the jurisdiction of the BOA. Accordingly, when the athlete, Jason Livingstone, tested positive for an anabolic steroid at the Barcelona Olympics, the British Athletic Federation (BAF) referred the results to the BOA, and arrangements were made to send him home. Livingstone has only recently returned to competition following a four-year ban.

Familiar substances which are proscribed by the Misuse of Drugs Act 1971 usually present few problems in detection. Random testing by the Football Association has caught out a number of young professional footballers, most cases involving so-called "recreational" drugs such as marijuana and speed. In fact, drug-testing in sport is not a recent development. In his autobiography, Jack Charlton tells how he was asked to provide urine samples after no less than four of England's six games in the 1966 World Cup. After the final, the doctors presented him with a hat on which they had written "For one who gave his best for England – the Jimmy Riddle Trophy". More seriously, in 1996 the Sussex cricketer, Ed Giddins, was banned by the Test and County Cricket Club and released by his county for alleged cocaine abuse. The greatest difficulty in recent times has been the differing clinical attitudes taken towards preparations which have "ambivalent" qualities (*i.e.* which are capable of performance-enhancing as well as providing a medicinal benefit). As *Drugs and Sport* points out, new pharmaceutical products are being developed continually and, consequently, no list of banned or permitted drugs can be absolutely complete. Thus, when two British weightlifters were sent home from the Barcelona Olympics in 1992 after testing positive for the compound Clenbuterol, opposing emminent clinical opinions were expressed as to the status of the substance. The two men, Andrew Saxton and Andrew Davies, claimed that they had unwittingly taken it as an ingredient in a cold preparation.

The arguments intensified when the golden girl of German athletics, Katrin Krabbe, and her compatriot, Grit Bruer, also tested positive for Clenbuterol. The substance did not appear on the IOC Medical Commission's list of banned products but, since it was reported as an anabolic agent, the IOC claimed that it qualified as a banned stimulant. However, to justify the ultimate sanction of depriving an athlete of his career, it surely cannot be good enough to say that he broke an unwritten, as opposed to an express, rule. Krabbe successfully overturned one ban imposed on her by the International Amateur Athletics Federation (IAAF) but, in late 1993, lost an appeal against a further ban relating to her alleged use of Clenbuterol. Further protracted litigation then took place, and in March 1996 a Munich Appeals Court found that she intentionally took another banned substance, Spiropent, over a long period in order to improve her athletic performance, without a doctor's prescription and without being ill. Krabbe had claimed that she took the substance to improve her breathing. Her fall from grace has intensified speculation over the astonishing performances of Chinese athletes and swimmers under the tutelage of coaches from the former East Germany.

The protracted Krabbe litigation represents the highwater mark of legal challenges made by athletes against bans imposed for the prohibited use of steroids. The failed application for declaratory relief by the Swiss athlete Sandra Gasser in 1988, was based on a restraint of trade argument. Gasser brought proceedings in the Chancery Division of the High Court after she was suspended for two years by the IAAF following a positive drugs test at the 1987 World Athletics Championships in Rome. Scott J indicated that the findings made by the Arbitration Panel of the IAAF in relation to the athlete's urine samples could not be impugned unless it could be shown that the Panel had exceeded its jurisdiction (which it had not, in his judgment). In other words, the fact that the Panel may have erred in making certain findings, or in the procedures which it had adopted, was irrelevant, provided it had not exceeded its terms of reference. Additionally, by the time Gasser applied to the High

Court, any remedy which she may have had under the Arbitration Acts was time-barred (see also Chapter 10, "Remedies").

Ben Johnson and the Dubin Inquiry into Drugs and Banned Practices in Sport

Perhaps the most infamous cheat of all was Ben Johnson, who streaked to victory in the men's 100m final at the 1988 Seoul Olympics in a world record time, only to be stripped of his gold medal when tests on a urine sample revealed the presence of the banned substance Stanozolol. The joy with which Johnson's victory was greeted in his adopted country, Canada, was quickly replaced by disbelief and national humiliation. In the aftermath of Johnson's ban, the Canadian Government ordered a commission of inquiry into the affair headed by its Chief Justice, the Honourable Charles Dubin. The report contained the damning indictment cited at the beginning of this section. He went on to conclude that the use of drugs as a method of cheating had reached "epidemic proportions". During the inquiry it emerged that the abuse of anabolic steroids was widespread and was no respecter of national boundaries: half the gold medallists in the US men's track team had used steroids which, in certain cases, had actually been prescribed to athletes. The inquiry rejected claims made by those acting for Johnson that there had been flaws in the testing procedures in Seoul, but recommended that in order to have a fair right of appeal, athletes should be in a position to be able to test the scientific validity of drug test results. In doing so, any doubt which may have existed over the application of a strict liability standard in doping cases appeared to have been removed. The Court of Arbitration for Sport (CAS) has recognised that even if the regulations of a governing body do not provide that a positive doping test can be rebutted by proof of absence of knowledge or intent regarding the taking of a banned substance, the accused has that right (see *G v FEI*, Case CAS 92/63).

The Modahl Case

On 26 July 1995 the Independent Appeal Tribunal set up by the BAF allowed the appeal of the British athlete Diane Modahl, who had earlier been banned from competition by a disciplinary committee of the BAF. At a meeting in Lisbon, Portugal on 18 June 1994 Modahl had provided a urine sample which, when tested, revealed the presence of testosterone seven times higher than the maximum permissible ratio under IAAF regulations. At the appeal hearing it was accepted by the BAF that it shouldered the burden of proving beyond a reasonable doubt that Modahl had committed the alleged doping offence (*i.e.* to the criminal standard of proof). On her behalf, a number of criticisms were levelled at the Portugese laboratory which handled and tested the offending sample, but these were rejected by the Appeal Panel, headed by Robert Reid QC. The ground upon which the appeal succeeded was the possibility that Modahl's urine sample had degraded by bacterial action due to it being stored in unrefrigerated conditions for a period of time, and that this had resulted in an increase in the level of testosterone found in the sample. The flawed aspect of the procedure broke one of the important links in the chain of custody intended to ensure that reliable test results are obtained (and thus reduce the scope for impeaching them). Modahl was therefore eligible to be selected for the British team at the Atlanta Olympics. She was picked, but, like the vast majority of our athletes, failed to distinguish herself.

According to an article in the *Independent* on 1 April 1997 Modahl is now suing BAF for £500,000, representing alleged loss of earnings during the period of her ban. That figure pales into insignificance compared with the $27 million award made in favour of the US 400m runner and former world record-holder 'Butch' Reynolds in an Ohio state court following the reversal of a ban for alleged drug abuse. The award was subsequently overturned on appeal, but it underlines the potentially huge financial liability which administrators are exposed to in the brave new world of professional athletics. It cannot be any coincidence that the IOC set up an *ad hoc* panel of the CAS to preside over the Atlanta Olympic Games. The cases which have been cited, and their highly damaging effect on the image of sport, reinforces the requirement to ensure that effective communication exists between doctors, athletes and governing bodies in order to provide an environment in which certainty and consistency prevails. At the same time, the need to preserve vital evidence and observe the principles of natural justice is the province of lawyers who will not always occupy the neutral corner of the ring. Until that position is reached, the cheats will continue to prosper and genuine athletes who unexpectedly excel will be subjected to the kind of whispering campaign which cast a shadow over the genuine achievements of the Irish swimmer Michelle Smith at Atlanta. Regrettably, the soul-searching which took place in Canada following the shame of Seoul did not move Ben Johnson sufficiently to prevent him from being banned for a second doping offence in

March 1993. Johnson's continued reliance on illegal substances, despite the intense glare of publicity, surely demonstrates how deep the drug culture runs and that the Dubin report's use of the word "epidemic" was no exaggeration.

Wilander v Tobin – a long rally

At the time of writing, the tennis players Mats Wilander and Karel Novacek are fighting the right of the International Tennis Federation (ITF) to test and ban players for drugs, in the High Court. So far, much heat has been generated by the players' application to amend their statement of claim to argue that rule 53 of the ITF's Rules, which govern drug testing in the sport, is in breach of Article 7 of the Anti-Doping Convention 1989. Under rule 53 a player becomes subject to mandatory penalties if the ITF Review Board, to which positive urine samples are submitted, finds that the rule has been violated. There is no right to raise a defence to a drugs charge unless an appeal is brought before the ITF's Appeals Committee whose decision is final. Wilander and Novacek argued that rule 53 failed to provide an appeals procedure, contrary to Article 7, and also breached Article 59 of the Treaty of Rome in that it restricted their freedom to provide services. They initially succeeded with their application to amend, but the Court of Appeal allowed the defendants' appeal (see *Wilander and another* v *Tobin and another (No 2)* (1997) *The Independent*, 24 January 1997; reversing Lightman J (1996) *The Times*, 15 July).

The Master of the Rolls, Lord Woolf, ruled that rule 53 was not incompatible with EU law, or the 1989 Convention, as the guilt or innocence of a player was determined by the laboratory test result and not by the Appeals Committee. A differently constituted Court of Appeal had already ruled in April 1996 that it was neither unfair nor unreasonable for rule 53 to reverse the normal burden of proof by requiring a player who had tested positive for drugs to prove his innocence on a balance of probabilities (see *Wilander* v *Tobin* (1996) *The Times*, 8 April). That is a different approach to the one taken by the BAF in the Modahl appeal, and underlines the fact that there is no single, uniform application of the burden of proof in drugs cases. It is hardly a recipe for certainty – the prosecution bearing the burden of proof to the criminal standard in one sport and the defence shouldering the burden to the civil standard in another. Moreover, the judgment of Lord Woolf in the most recent visit of the *Wilander* case to the Court of Appeal appears to condone a strict liability approach to drug-testing. He also found that the powers of the High Court to review the appeals procedure provided the necessary safeguards required by Article 7 of the 1989 Convention. However, if, by the use of the word "review", Lord Woolf means an application under Rules of the Supreme Court Ord 53, then that procedure has clearly been shown to provide an aggrieved party with no safeguards whatsoever (see Chapter 10, "Remedies").

The hidden dangers of drug-taking

Much of what has been said in this chapter may appear only to concern those who reach the very pinnacle of their particular sport. High-profile cases are newsworthy, but drug abuse and inappropriate medication is not the exclusive preserve of professional sport. There are also product liability considerations which the drug-takers would do well to remember. The general principle is that when drugs are prescribed by a doctor he is deemed to be the supplier of the medication, and the drug company is the producer. If licenced drugs are lawfully prescribed for an exclusively medicinal purpose, the patient will have the full panoply of legal remedies in the event that he suffers harmful side-effects as a result of taking such medication. However, if an athlete receives drugs which are illegal, or which are not supplied in a wholly medical context, the product liability safeguards will not apply. In that event the athlete will have to look to the person who supplied him with the drugs who, almost by definition, will be a charlatan and, quite possibly, a man of straw.

Two classes of licenced drug which are commonly available and which have performance-enhancing properties are Beta-agonists and Nsaid's. Beta-agonists, such as salbutamol and Clenbuterol, are prescription drugs which are used as a treatment for asthma and in other cold remedies. Their principal function is to dilate the respiratory tract and thus aid breathing. However, they also affect the cardio-vascular system by increasing the heart rate and pumping more blood around the body, thus enhancing performance. The potential side-effects include abnormal heart rate, irregular heart rhythm and, if taken in large enough quantities, symptoms mimicking a heart attack. Nsaid's are non-steroidal, anti-inflammatory drugs which can be purchased over the counter in any pharmacy. They include drugs such as aspirin and ibuprofen which are not normally associated with abuse or increased performance. What they are capable of is artificially enhancing pain tolerance and so facilitate more strenuous and prolonged exercise. However, taking such drugs in large quantities can cause serious stomach problems, including ulcers, as well as increasing the susceptibility to allergies. The other consequence is, of course, that all the time the pain is simply being masked, which means that the underlying condition is being aggravated.

To reiterate the point that has already been made, if either class of drug is taken for non-medicinal purposes, and harmful side-effects occur, the manufacturer will almost certainly repudiate liability. That is quite apart from the fact that Beta-agonists now appear on every respectable sport's banned list of substances, as do the more sophisticated Nsaid's. Accordingly, an athlete who is handed an unmarked bottle of drugs is well advised to establish the precise nature of its contents, their origins, the purpose of the drugs, any side-effects, and whether they contain any banned substances. Great care should also be taken with certain traditional preparations – as some have found to their cost.

Chapter 10

Remedies

Introduction

Claims with a sporting theme are capable of touching nearly every corner of the law, and it is therefore beyond the scope of this book to do any more than simply to identify the main remedies available to an aggrieved party. For a more detailed exposition on the subject, the reader should refer to *MacGregor on Damages*, *Clerk & Lindsell on Torts*, and *Chitty on Contracts*. In the majority of cases that practitioners are likely to encounter on a day-to-day basis, the client's main objective will be to obtain compensation for injuries and other losses he has suffered through his involvement in sport. In addition to considering the recovery of damages, this chapter also sets out, in some detail, the procedure for making an application for compensation to the Criminal Injuries Compensation Authority, and charts the unsuccessful attempts that have been made to invoke the judicial review machinery against the governing bodies of sport. Finally, more informal methods of dispute resolution, such as arbitration and the various methods of alternative dispute resolution, are discussed.

Identifying who to sue

A discussion of the potential remedies available to a claimant presupposes that the party or parties responsible for alleged loss and damage arising out of a sporting accident, breach of contract or some other wrong have been correctly identified. That task may require great care and consideration in certain cases. This is particularly true where spectators are injured, and potential defendants might include the participants, the organiser of the event, the occupier of the venue (if different to the organiser), other spectators, the police and other rescue services. The litigation arising out of the Hillsborough disaster could have been a contemporary and vivid example of the difficulties involved, were it not for the admitted negligence of the Chief Constable of South Yorkshire.

Vicarious liability

If the alleged tortfeasor were playing in a game in the course of his employment, his employer will be vicariously liable for his actions in accordance with the established legal principles, and can be sued as co-defendant. An employer would not be so liable for a player's deliberate assault unless it had encouraged its employee to commit the assault. Accordingly, alleging assault without pleading negligence in the alternative simply plays into the hands of an employer who had no control or influence over a deliberate assault committed by its employee ostensibly in the course of his employment. As a general rule, if an employee is required to take part in a sporting activity by his employer then the activity will be regarded as part of his employment; it is immaterial that the activity takes place outside normal working hours. On the other hand, a member of a staff works team, playing for enjoyment after work, would probably not be regarded as acting in the course of his employment. It has been noted in Chapter 2 that vicarious liability can also arise in the context of an unincorporated association, such as a club (see *Brown* v *Lewis* (1896) 12 TLR 455).

Two or more potential defendants

As far as participants in a sport or game are concerned, the potential tortfeasors will probably be readily ascertainable, especially where the claim is brought by player against player. In other cases, difficult choices may need to be made, as the case of *Harrison* v *Vincent* [1982] RTR 8 illustrates. The plaintiff was a side-car passenger who was injured when the motorcycle and side-car on which he was riding crashed at a hairpin bend during a race, colliding with a recovery vehicle. The rear brake had failed and the driver then missed a gear in an attempt to slow the bike down. The plaintiff sued:

- those responsible for the negligent assembly of the brake mechanism; and
- the organisers of the event for the negligent positioning of the recovery vehicle which was obstructing an escape route.

No claim was brought against the rider of the motorcycle. Both defendants were found liable and their appeals were dismissed. Having succeeded against both, the plaintiff was then at liberty to recover his entire damages award from just one of them under the joint torfeasors principle. In *Harrison* the plaintiff made the right judgment in who to sue, but the perennial problem associated with suing two or more defendants is the costs implications involved if the claim succeeds against some but not all the dependants. Unfortunately, that is simply a hazard of litigation and there is little practical advice of general application that can be given.

Damages

Whether a claim arises out of an injury sustained whilst participating in sport or attending at a sporting event, a breach of contract, or some other cause of action, the claim will most likely proceed by way of ordinary action. The choice of venue will be dictated by the value of the claim, and the procedure for determining how much a claim is worth is explained in Chapter 11. Suffice it to say here that personal injury claims should only be commenced in the High Court where, at the outset, the plaintiff's solicitor is able to certify that the claim is worth at least £50,000. The new financial limits which have to be stated on summonses issued in a county court will require greater care to be taken in assessing the likely value of a claim. The huge increase in the cost of commencing proceedings is intended to make the county courts self-financing. At the time of writing, the consensus appears to be that if a claim turns out to be worth more than the limit stated on the face of the summons the plaintiff will not be restricted to that figure, but will be able to amend his claim on condition that he pays the difference in issue fees.

General damages

Pain, suffering and loss of amenity

In a personal injury case the starting-point for assessing the value of general damages for pain, suffering and loss of amenity should be the Judicial Studies Board Guidelines. Once the broad parameters of the likely award are established, they can then usually be narrowed down by reference to cases in *Kemp & Kemp, Butterworths Personal Injury Litigation Service* and *Current Law*. Some of the comparators have a sporting theme: for example, in *May v Strong* [1991] BPILS [2274], an award of £6,000 was made to a semi-professional footballer who suffered a compound fracture of his fibula and tibia as a result of a very late tackle from behind. It is interesting to note that the trial judge found that the recklessness of the defendant was so great that the tackle amounted to an assault. The award would be worth approximately £7,600 in 1997, although the religious application of inflation multipliers can have a distorting effect on awards made in old cases, and an attempt should therefore be made to locate the most recent comparators.

Provisional damages

It is good practice for those acting for plaintiffs to consider from the very outset of a claim whether it is appropriate to apply for provisional damages under RSC Order 37, rules 7 to 10 (applied in the county courts under CCR Ord 22, r 6A). A provisional award assumes that the plaintiff will *not* suffer a serious deterioration, but the order will entitle him to apply to the court for a further award in the event that he does. Two conditions must be satisfied for a court to make such an award:

(1) the so-called "chance" condition; and
(2) a finding that there is a substantial risk that the plaintiff will, at some time in the future, suffer a serious deterioration in his physical or mental condition due to the defendant's negligence.

In practice, the chance must be capable of quantification ("more than merely fanciful") and, accordingly, a 2% to 3% risk of a plaintiff developing malignant mesothelioma has been held to satisfy the condition (see *Patterson* v *Ministry of Defence*, cited in *Kemp & Kemp* para 12-271). The second requirement is often much more difficult to fulfil. The deterioration must be out of the ordinary in the sense that it is clearly severable and not merely the natural progression of the condition in question. A medical report which addresses the two factors is, of course, essential. It is also necessary to plead accurately the facts relied on in support of a claim for provisional damages. From a tactical standpoint it is worth bearing in mind that insurers recoil at the prospect of having to keep a file open indefinitely. Consequently, a more favourable, once-and-for-all settlement can often be obtained in cases where the spectre of provisional damages is raised.

Handicap in the labour market

If a plaintiff is able to return to work following an accident, but is likely to find himself on the labour market prior to normal retirement age due to residual symptoms, he is prima facie entitled to a further award to compensate him for his disadvantage in the labour market. There is no particular science to the assessment of so-called *Smith* v *Manchester* awards (*Smith* v *Manchester Corporation* [1974] 17 KIR 1), but some judges use one year's net loss of earnings as a convenient yardstick, and then make adjustments according to various other factors such as the plaintiff's age, qualifications and skills, together with employment trends and the state of the local and national labour market at the time of the hearing. The estimated time-scale within which the plaintiff is likely to find himself on the job market is, of course, another critical consideration. In an appropriate case the services of an employment consultant may be required. Awards of five figures are rare, and if real uncertainty exists over a plaintiff's job prospects, serious consideration should be given to the suitability of making an application for provisional damages and thus for the claim to be reopened at a future date.

Special damages

In many cases the largest single item of loss will be the earnings which the plaintiff has lost due to an enforced absence from work. Where there is a consistent pattern of earnings prior to the accident, quantification should be straightforward. Self-employed plaintiffs can present difficulties, especially where their earnings fluctuate and no discernible pattern emerges. In either case, a chequered work history punctuated by periods of unemployment or absence from work due to health reasons can also cause complications. Future loss of earnings are, to a greater or lesser extent, speculative in that they depend on the assumption that an existing state of affairs will continue. However, what happens when a court is called upon to assess the likelihood of a certain contingency occurring which did not exist at the time the injury or other damage was caused? For example, an amateur footballer with aspirations of turning professional might be prevented from fulfilling his potential by a foot injury in an accident caused by the defendant's negligence. In *Mulvain and another* v *Joseph and another* (1968) 112 SJ 927, an American club professional golfer injured his hand as a result of a taxi driver's negligence. He was awarded damages for the lost opportunity to compete in tournaments, the loss of experience and prestige which might have resulted from him becoming a tournament professional, and the lost chance of winning prize money. A similar task confronted Holland J in *Bobby* v *Bird Construction Ltd* (1988) (unreported) where the plaintiff was a top, amateur darts player with aspirations of becoming a professional. In such cases an element of crystal ball gazing needs to be employed, but the court is required to make a judgment despite the difficulties involved.

Damages for breach of contract

It is beyond the scope of this book to do anything more than state the most basic legal principles applicable to damages for breach of contract. An award of damages is the usual remedy for a defendant's breach of a contractual undertaking. Compensatory damages may be substantial in order to put the plaintiff in the position he would have been in if the defendant had honoured his obligations or, if the plaintiff cannot show that he has suffered an actual loss, a nominal award will be made. The types of loss for which compensation is awarded include straightforward pecuniary loss (*e.g.* the additional fee due to Bournemouth FC following the transfer of Ted MacDougall to Manchester United), physical inconvenience and, in certain limited circumstances, distress. Damages for loss of reputation are not generally recoverable in contract unless the purpose of the agreement was to enhance an existing reputation. In an appropriate case, the better course will be to claim damages for distress and anxiety, but apart from holidays with a sporting theme it is unlikely that a sports-related contract would have, as its underlying purpose, the relief of stress or providing peace of mind (see *Jarvis* v *Swan Tours Ltd* [1973] QB 233 and *Jackson* v *Horizon Holidays* [1975] 1 WLR 1468). However, a player who suffers distress as a consequence of his club's breach of contract may be able to pursue such a claim by analogy with *Cox* v *Philips Industries* [1976] 1 WLR 638. Since damages for breach of contract are compensatory and are not intended to punish a defendant, exemplary damages are not available even if the defendant's motives are shown to have been bad.

Equitable remedies

The equitable remedies of injunction, specific performance and rescission are available to an aggrieved plaintiff, depending on the particular circumstances of the case and the relief sought. The availability of a mandatory or prohibitory injunction in cases where the defendant is alleged to have committed a continuing nuisance has already been discussed in Chapter 4. The judgments of the Court of Appeal in *Kennaway* v *Thompson* (above) show the approach which the courts adopt to such applications. The injunction recently granted to Mark Jones, the Welsh Rugby Union player, against the Welsh RU shows that the courts are prepared to grant interlocutory relief to a player aggrieved by disciplinary sanctions imposed on him by his sporting body (*Jones and another* v *Welsh Rugby Football Union* (1997) *The Times*, 6 March). The injunction in the *Jones* case was positive, in the sense that it allowed him to continue to play rugby pending his appeal against the ban imposed. Specific performance and rescission will arise exclusively in the context of contractual disputes, and the usual principles will apply to all forms of equitable relief, including the requirement that the plaintiff has "clean hands". The courts will not, as a general rule, compel the performance of contracts of employment against the will of either the employer or employee, and in such a case the aggrieved party's remedy lies in damages alone. Accordingly, a player who refuses to appear for the club to whom he is contracted may be in repudiatory breach of contract, but he cannot be forced to play.

Private prosecution

If a criminal offence is alleged to have taken place, but the police or Crown Prosecution Service decline to pursue the matter, it is open to the aggrieved party to bring a private prosecution. However, it has already been noted that a criminal court does not have the machinery to award the kind of compensation available in the civil courts.

Compensating victims of criminal violence

Almost by definition, the perpetrator of an act of criminal violence will not have the wherewithal to compensate his victim for any injuries sustained by him. The criminal courts can order a defendant to pay compensation (under s 35 of the Powers of Criminal Courts Act 1975) but, unless the victim's injuries are very minor, such an order is unlikely to provide the victim with adequate recompense. Moreover, this assumes that the perpetrator is apprehended. Even then, the police or Crown Prosecution Service may decline to pursue the matter. In all those situations, often the only remedy available to the aggrieved party is to make an application for compensation to the Criminal Injuries Compensation Authority (CICA), formerly the Criminal Injuries Compensation Board (CICB). Applications which are received by CICA on or after 1 April 1996 fall to be considered under the 1996 scheme, which was introduced by the Criminal Injuries Compensation Act 1995.

Criminal Injuries Compensation Scheme – 1996 scheme

The persons who are prima facie entitled to claim under the scheme are those who have sustained personal injury which is directly attributable to a crime of violence, or have suffered injury attributable to the apprehension (or attempted apprehension) of an offender (or suspected offender), or the prevention (or attempted prevention) of an offence, or in giving assistance to the police. An application can also be made by dependants and relatives of a person who has died as a consequence of criminal injuries. Indeed, as has been noted, it may be the only option available to someone who has been attacked by an impecunious assailant. The criteria by which CICA assesses applications, and its practice and procedure, are reproduced in full in Part XVI of Butterworths *Personal Injury Litigation Service* (the 1990 scheme, under which pre-April 1996 applications are determined, can also be found in the same section). The principal features of the 1996 scheme to note are as follows:

"Criminal injury"

Under paragraph 8, "criminal injury" includes:

- a crime of violence (including arson, fire-raising or an act of poisoning); or
- an offence of trespass on a railway; or
- the apprehension or attempted apprehension of an offender or a suspected offender, the prevention or attempted prevention of an offence, or the giving of help to any constable who is engaged in any such activity.

"Personal injury"

For the purposes of the new scheme, "personal injury" is defined in paragraph 9 to include both physical injury (including fatal injury) and mental injury (a medically recognised illness or condition). If the claim is in respect of mental injury alone (*i.e.* it does not result directly from any physical injury), compensation will not be paid unless the applicant:

- was put in immediate physical harm to his own person; or
- had a close relationship of love and affection with another person when that person sustained physical injury (including death) as a direct consequence of any conduct referred to in paragraph 8, and:

- the relationship is continuing (unless the victim has died); and
- the applicant either witnessed and was present when the other person sustained the injury, or was closely involved in its immediate aftermath.

There are two further categories which are not relevant for present purposes. It can be seen how the qualifying criteria closely follow the legal principles which have developed from the "nervous shock" cases (*e.g. McLoughlin* v *O'Brian* [1983] 1 AC 410).

The other main points to note are as follows:

- It is not necessary for the assailant to have been convicted of a criminal offence in connection with the injury for the victim to bring a claim (para 10).
- A personal injury is not deemed to be a criminal injury for the purposes of the scheme where the injury is attributable to a vehicle, except where the vehicle was used deliberately to inflict, or in an attempt to inflict, injury (para 11). This excludes the victims of careless driving from pursuing claims.
- **The time-limit for bringing a claim is now reduced from three to two years** (para 17). This very important change is liable to catch out the unwary and those who proceed on the mistaken assumption that the usual three-year limitation period for bringing a personal injury claim applies. The time-limit can be waived at the discretion of the claims officer assigned to the case, but it is clearly far preferable to avoid having to rely on that indulgence.
- The minimum award is £1,000 for applications received after 1 April 1996 (a level 1 award).
- Awards of general damages are tariff-based, the tariff providing a description of each injury.
- Claims for loss of earnings and other consequential losses can now be made (although the first 28 weeks' loss of earnings cannot be recovered (para 30). Additionally, compensation for net loss of earnings is limited to one-and-a-half times the gross average UK industrial wage at the date of assessment as published by the *Department of Employment Gazette* and adjusted by CICA in its discretion (para 34).
- The latest scheme does not provide compensation for loss of, or damage to, clothing or other property, unless it is relied on by the victim as a physical aid, and even then the applicant must have either lost earnings or been incapacitated for more

than 28 weeks following the infliction of the injury complained of (para 25 – "Compensation for special expenses").

- Recoupable state benefits are deducted in full and pension payments *may* be deducted.
- In fatal accident cases, if the victim dies in consequence of his injuries no compensation other than reasonable funeral expenses can be recovered on behalf of his estate, although the minimum award does not apply in such a case (para 38). Claims for loss of dependency and bereavement *may* be recoverable in accordance with the provisions of the Fatal Accidents Act 1976 by those persons identified in paragraph 38 (up to a limit of £500,000).
- Interest is not payable on CICA awards.
- The procedure for reconsidering, reopening and reviewing decisions made by a claims officer appointed by CICA is set out in paragraphs 53 to 60 of the scheme. An applicant who is dissatisfied with a review decision, or the adequacy of an award, may apply for an oral hearing, which takes place before a panel of at least two adjudicators. An appellant is entitled to be legally represented, but the cost of such representation will not be recoverable from either CICA or the panel (see para 61 *et seq* for the various appeal procedures).

It should also be noted that an award may be withheld or reduced in certain circumstances. These are set out in paragraph 13 of the scheme and include:

- the applicant's failure to take, without delay, all reasonable steps to inform the police, or other body or person considered by the authority to be appropriate for the purpose, of the circumstances giving rise to the injury; or
- the applicant's failure to co-operate with the police or other authority in attempting to bring the assailant to justice; or
- the applicant's failure to give all reasonable assistance to the authority, or other body, or person in connection with the application; or
- the conduct of the applicant before, during or after the incident giving rise to the application, which renders it inappropriate to make a full or any award; or
- the applicant's character as shown by his criminal convictions (excluding convictions spent under the Rehabilitation of Offenders Act 1974), or by evidence available to the claims

officer which renders it inappropriate to make a full, or any, award.

The CICB reported that claims submitted by footballers and rugby players who had been assaulted during matches were frequently rejected because the victims either failed or delayed in reporting the incident to the police. Historically, the requirement to report an incident has been rigorously enforced by the CICB as it is often difficult to distinguish between negligent and criminal conduct. Many applicants appear to conclude that incidents are not worth reporting because no action will be taken. In many instances they are probably right, but that is not the point as far as CICA is concerned, and there is no reason to believe that it will soften the line taken by its predecessor. It is, therefore, crucial that incidents are reported to the police as soon as possible. A claimant must then assist in any prosecution which is brought. Each case is judged on its own merits, but the conduct and character of the applicant is assessed, and an award may be refused if he is found to have been responsible in some way for his injuries.

The evidence-gathering exercise in pursuance of making an application to CICA should be carried out in the same way as the preparation of any other personal injury claim. The procedure for making a claim can be found in paragraph 17 of the scheme. CICA publishes guideline figures for damages in respect of specific injuries which appear, *inter alia*, in *Kemp & Kemp*, *Current Law* and *Butterworths Personal Injury Litigation Service*. The criticism levelled at the CICB from time to time was that its awards tended to be lower than those made by the civil courts. Whether there is any hard evidence to support that theory is debatable, but the victim who would otherwise be left empty-handed surely cannot be heard to complain. That observation applies just as much in the context of sport as it does in any other social setting. Indeed, the scheme is a shining example of how collective responsibility operates in a fair and just society.

Judicial review

The decisions of the larger governing bodies of sport often have a marked effect on a large section of the public, and it has been observed that some bodies, such as the Football Association and the Jockey Club, enjoy virtual monopolies. However, both the Divisional Court and the Court of Appeal have repeatedly declined to allow the decisions of sporting bodies to be challenged by way of proceedings for judicial review under RSC Order 53, although applications for injunctive relief in private law actions have met with more success (see *e.g. Jones* v *Welsh Rugby Union* (above)). The *Datafin* decision, which widened the scope of judicial review to include bodies other than those created by statute, has not led to sporting bodies being successfully challenged for their administrative acts (*R* v *Panel on Take-Overs and Mergers, ex parte Datafin* [1987] QB 815). On the contrary, the courts have adopted an essentially "hands-off", non-interventionist approach to such challenges, justifying their stance on the ground that sporting bodies are domestic institutions, rather than public bodies, whose powers arise from (and duties exist) in private law only.

Law v National Greyhound Racing Club

The immunity of sport's governing bodies from judicial review can be traced back to the pre-*Datafin* decision of *Law* v *National Greyhound Racing Club Ltd* [1983] 3 All ER 300, albeit a private law action. The defendant was a limited company and the governing body for greyhound racing in Great Britain. The plaintiff was a trainer whose licence had been suspended by the respondent following a positive doping test on one of his greyhounds. The plaintiff sought a declaration that the stewards' decision was void and ultra vires. The Court of Appeal rejected the defendant's contention that the claim was susceptible to judicial review on the following grounds:

- the stewards' powers were derived from a contract, and a stewards' enquiry only concerned those who voluntarily submitted to its jurisdiction. There was no public element in that jurisdiction, even though the stewards' powers did affect the public;
- the defendant's authority to perform judicial or *quasi*-judicial functions in respect of those to whom it had granted licences was not derived from statute, statutory instrument or the Crown. Accordingly, in exercising its powers such a body is in the nature of a domestic, rather than a public, tribunal.

Post-Law

In subsequent cases the courts have felt bound by the ruling in *Law*, although certain judicial comments suggest that the door may not be closed for good. In R v *Disciplinary Committee of the Jockey Club ex parte Massingberd-Mundy* (1990) *The Times*, 3 January the applicant sought judicial review, on the grounds of a failure of natural justice, following the Jockey Club's decision to remove his name from a list of those qualified to act as chairman of a panel of local stewards. The Divisional Court indicated that if it were not bound by earlier authority, it might well have concluded that at least some of the Jockey Club's decisions were amenable to judicial review. However, the comments were *obiter* since the issue which arose in the case had no public element at all. The decision in *Massingberd-Mundy* was criticised (but followed) in R v *Jockey Club ex parte Ram Racecourses Ltd* [1991] COD 346, where a differently constituted Divisional Court said that *Law* could have been distinguished in the light of the *Datafin* decision. Simon Brown J expressed the view that the Jockey Club ought to be subject to judicial review when it exercised certain functions, such as its licensing powers. The precedent set in *Law* was once again applied in R v *Football Association of Wales ex parte Flint Town United Football Club* [1991] COD 4. In that case a contractual relationship existed between the parties giving rise to private law rights, and it was therefore not possible to distinguish *Law* in the manner suggested by the court in the *Ram Racecourses* case.

Attempts to challenge the decisions of football's governing bodies

In the past five years football's governing bodies have found themselves embroiled in High Court litigation and, in the first instance, locked horns together in R v *Football Association Ltd ex parte Football League Ltd* [1993] 2 All ER 833. The League sought judicial review of the FA's decision to create the new Premier League for the 1992/93 football season. The League contended that a potential conflict of interest would arise if the FA, as a regulating body, entered into commercial competition with the League by running its own competition. The FA issued a cross-application seeking declarations that (1) the FA was not a body susceptible to judicial review either in general or, more particularly, at the instigation of the League with whom it was contractually bound; and (2) it was impossible, in any event, to construe the establishment of the Premier League as frustrating the policy of the enabling instrument, or as being contrary to its true intent or meaning. Rose J held that despite the virtual monopoly it enjoyed, and the importance of its decisions to many members of the public, the FA was a domestic body whose powers arose, and duties existed, in private law only. It was not underpinned directly or indirectly by any organ or agency of the state, or any potential government interest. Accordingly, it was inappropriate to apply principles designed to control abuse of power by government. The League's application was therefore dismissed and the FA was granted the declaratory relief it sought.

There then followed two private (as opposed to public) law actions (*i.e.* outside the scope of RSC Ord 53). In 1995 three semi-professional Welsh football clubs claimed declaratory and injunctive relief against their governing body, the Football Association of Wales (FAW), on the ground of restraint of trade. A resolution of the FAW compelled the clubs, who were based in Wales, to play at the grounds of English clubs instead of on their home grounds. Jacob J found that FAW had acted in unreasonable restraint of trade by enforcing an arrangement on the clubs which was damaging to their trade (see *Newport Association Football Club Ltd* v *Football Association of Wales Ltd* [1995] 2 All ER 87 (for a fuller discussion of the case, see Chapter 8).

The Football League found itself in the legal spotlight again after Stevenage Borough FC finished top of the GM Vauxhall Conference league for the 1995/96 season. That success prima facie entitled the club to be promoted to the third division of the Nationwide Football League. However, the club did not satisfy certain requirements of the Football League which had to be complied with by the end of December in the previous year, principally those relating to stadium capacity and financial criteria. Stevenage expected to be able to satisfy the League's criteria by the commencement of the new season in August. When the club was refused entry to the League, it challenged the criteria on the ground that they amounted to a restraint of trade and were unreasonable, and sought a declaration that it was entitled to be promoted. The application was dismissed, both at first instance and following an expedited appeal, on the ground that it had been made too late. This was despite the obvious fact that none of the clubs in the Conference League knew whether they would win promotion by the date the League's criteria had to be satisfied. It is clear, however, from the judgment of Carnwath J that if the League's rules were shown to be arbitrary or capricious they were open to review by the courts, the burden of proof lying with the party seeking to establish that that was the case. The judge's distinction between the private and public aspect of the relationship between the club and the League, and the wider implications of the latter, are also interesting to note.

The Court of Appeal emphasised that the issue was whether the rules for promotion to, and relegation from, the League were valid, not simply whether Stevenage should have been promoted. To that end, there were said to be three relevant questions when considering a challenge to the rules of the Football League, namely (1) whether any and, if so, which of the rules were invalid; (2) if so, whether it should grant a declaration to that effect; and (3) if so, whether it should make an order, by way of an injunction or declaration, giving effect to the modified rules after those found to be invalid had been excised. Furthermore, even where the court was satisfied that each of those questions were answered affirmatively, it would be an exceptional case in which it would be right to give retrospective effect to the modified rules (see *Stevenage Borough Football Club Ltd* v *The Football League Ltd* (1996) *The Times*, 1 August; (1996) *The Times*, 9 August CA).

The fixture pile-up at the end of the 1996/97 Premier League campaign has led to clubs which are heavily involved in cup competitions threatening legal action against the FA for refusing to extend the season. Apart from underlining the "sue at the drop of a hat" tendency, any action would probably fail on one of the grounds which thwarted Stevenage Borough's claim, namely that the courts will not interfere with a governing body's rules once a season has started. In the wider context, Stevenage's failure to win promotion to the third division of the Football League was the third such failure in as many years. At the same time, many clubs in the second and third divisions of the League are running at a financial deficit and would not meet the League's criteria for promotion from the Conference League. Clubs also have until 1998 to make ground improvements in order to meet the requirements of the Taylor report, yet the club which has finished top of the Conference League for the past three seasons has been expected to satisfy those requirements with immediate effect. One could be forgiven for concluding that the rules are not being applied in an even-handed manner, although the courts do not appear to have seen it that way.

The Aga Khan and the Jockey Club

In 1989 the Aga Khan failed in his attempt to obtain judicial review of the Jockey Club's decision to disqualify his horse, Aliysa, from one of the English Classic races for an alleged doping offence (see *R v Jockey Club, ex parte The Aga Khan* (1992) *The Times*, 9 December). The Court of Appeal reiterated that whilst the Jockey Club exercised broad and monopolistic powers over a significant national activity, it was not in its origin, history, constitution and membership, a public body. Its powers were derived from the consent of owners to abide by the rules of racing according to the Court. The Aga Khan subsequently withdrew his string of horses from training in this country, and has only recently returned to race here.

A private law remedy?

It has also been shown that the courts are prepared to interfere where disciplinary procedures contravene the rules of natural justice (although a finding that a contractual relationship existed appears to have been material to the judicial intervention in both *Wilander and another v Tobin and another (No 2)* (1996) *The Times*, 15 July, and *Jones v Welsh Rugby Union* (above)). In *Wilander* Lightman J ruled that the International Tennis Federation Rules were arguably invalid because of their failure to respect the fundamental rights of sportsmen to a fair hearing only to be overturned by the Court of Appeal. Indeed, where privity of contract exists between an aggrieved party and one of the sporting "monopolies" under discussion, he will have another remedy, and judicial review may be refused on that very ground. Alternatively, if a private law remedy is unavailable it would appear that there is nothing to stop the FA, the Jockey Club or any of the other bodies responsible for governing sport from acting in an arbitrary and capricious manner and very little that anyone aggrieved of such conduct can do about it. For example, in *Gasser v Stinson & another* (1988) (unreported), a Swiss athlete challenged a two-year ban imposed on her for a drugs offence by the International Amateur Athletic Federation on the grounds that it was unfair and unreasonable. Her claim was dismissed on the ground that the courts should be reluctant to allow an implied contractual obligation relating to fair treatment to be used as a means of judicially reviewing honest decisions of sport's governing bodies. In arriving at that decision the court said that those bodies are far better suited to judge such matters than the courts. That may be correct as a general rule, but it did not exclude Ebsworth J from granting the kind of interlocutory relief which an applicant would seek in an application for judicial review.

Conclusion

The judges of the Crown Office have, it is suggested, fallen into error by consistently treating the decision in *Law* v *National Greyhound Club* as binding authority when all cases decided prior to *Datafin* ought to be reviewed in the light of that landmark ruling. Furthermore, the reality is that bodies such as the Football Association and the Jockey Club now wield enormous powers. To determine whether they are susceptible to judicial review simply by reference to such arbitrary factors like whether they are creatures of statute misses the power point. When sporting bodies exercise functions which are exclusively regulatory in nature, the consensual element which thwarted the Aga Khan's application is missing. In those cases (the starkest example of which is *Ram*), the arguments in favour of the decisions of sporting bodies being reviewable are powerful. Moreover, as a matter of fairness and justice, it is difficult to see why an aggrieved party should be in a worse position simply because he has no privity of contract with his governing body, and the consensual element is missing. Regrettably, it seems as if the decision in *Law* will have to be tested by the House of Lords if there is going to be a material shift in the way in which the courts approach applications for judicial review against sport's governing bodies. The boundaries between the concepts of private and public law are not always easy to distinguish but, for the time being at least, a person who is aggrieved by the decision of a sporting body exercising either its *quasi* judicial (*i.e.* disciplinary) or regulatory powers will be compelled to pursue the more protracted route of a private law action provided, of course, that such an avenue is open to him.

Arbitration

The merits of the "litigate or arbitrate?" debate are discussed in Chapter 11. With effect from 8 January 1996 the small claims limit was increased to £3,000, although personal injury claims are excluded from the new threshold which remains at £1,000. In order to encourage litigants to conduct small claims themselves, and thereby save legal expenses, party and party costs orders are only made in those cases where it can be shown that the losing party has acted unreasonably. The involvement of lawyers should therefore be kept to a minimum. Indeed, as a general observation the question of costs often assumes far greater significance when dealing with claims of relatively low value. Accordingly, in such cases, more than any other, it is essential that a clear appraisal of the likely cost of the litigation is made from the outset so that the client can make a fully informed decision regarding the viability of suing. It is often difficult to give a precise estimate of costs, but a "ball-park" figure will avoid any criticism later from the client that he did not envisage that the claim would cost so much to prosecute/defend. The culture of predicting the value of a claim, and the likely expense of seeing the case through to its conclusion, is something to which the legal profession will have to adapt if that aspect of the Woolf proposals is implemented. It is a skill which those practitioners who have agreed to undertake instructions on a conditional fee basis are already having to adapt to for purely selfish reasons.

Alternative dispute resolution

In addition to the traditional methods of resolving disputes, other forms of resolving disagreements exist; these are principally arbitration and, to an increasing extent, alternative dispute resolution (ADR). The determination of a dispute by an expert is another option. ADR is intended to produce a speedy outcome in an informal, confidential and cost-effective manner. It is a particularly attractive option in cases involving an international dimension which invariably give rise to jurisdictional difficulties. In 1983 the International Olympic Committee set up the Court of Arbitration for Sport (CAS) which has been successful in resolving disputes between sportsmen and their governing bodies. In particular, the CAS has intervened in cases where the legality of bans imposed for drug-taking is challenged, an area which has achieved prominence in recent years. The success of the *ad hoc* panel of the CAS, which was established for the duration of the Atlanta Olympics, has already been noted in Chapter 9.

A key feature of ADR is that it is driven by the parties rather than a court, judge or arbitrator. It is therefore less adversarial in nature, which gives the parties an opportunity to maintain their relationship pending the outcome of the dispute. It takes a variety of different forms: the basic and most widely used method being negotiations between the parties themselves, with third parties becoming involved only in order to facilitate an exchange of ideas. The next tier of third-party involvement is mediation, where a neutral person encourages the parties to negotiate a settlement. However, a mediator does not have the power to bind the parties, whereas an adjudicator (*e.g.* an arbitrator or an expert) does. It is also open to the parties to agree a method for resolving a dispute which draws on aspects of the other methods discussed (a so-called "hybrid arrangement"). Finally, the parties can opt for a mini-trial, which involves each side delivering a concise statement of its case to executives of the other party to the dispute. This can often concentrate minds on settlement. If it is intended that ADR should be pursued in the event of a dispute, the contract between the parties should say so in clear terms.

Chapter 11

Practice and Procedure

Introduction

This chapter is designed to give practical and helpful advice and assistance in the preparation and successful prosecution of a claim or defence. The conduct of certain sport-related disputes may involve practice and procedure outside the mainstream of litigation, for example challenging the findings of a doping test, which will almost certainly require highly specialised evidence. A legal adviser may also have to acquaint himself with the internal procedures adopted by the particular sporting body concerned. Those cases apart, there is little, if any, difference between the conduct of sports-related litigation and any other form of legal action. The advice and tips which follow are written primarily from a plaintiff's standpoint, but many of the recommendations also hold good for defendants. The theme underpinning this chapter is that a successful case is built on solid foundations. It is often very difficult to put a claim together at the eleventh hour, and even if it can be done, adverse inferences may well be drawn by the court or tribunal. Badly prepared cases can be won, but too many cases which should be won are lost or prejudiced by inadequate preparation. Things can also go wrong due to a failure to observe procedural rules once a claim has commenced, and pointers are given to help avoid the embarrassment of that happening.

The following is no substitute for a thorough knowledge of the relevant procedural rules, whether it is the Rules of Supreme Court, the County Court Rules, or internal rules promulgated by the sporting body in question. Another critical consideration at the very outset of a claim is to determine the appropriate forum in which to bring a claim. This may be complicated if the case has an international dimension (*e.g.* one or both of the parties is ordinarily resident outside of the jurisdiction, in which case consideration should be given to the application of the Civil Jurisdiction and Judgments Act 1982 and international Conventions). Although the traditional method of litigating disputes is recognised as being slow, complex and expensive, there are certain cases which ought to be tried by that process: the first is where the internal rules of the sport in question are incapable of providing the plaintiff with adequate compensation, or other redress, for the loss or damage he has suffered; the second is where the court is skilled in dealing with the subject-matter of the claim, such as copyright, trademarks and other intellectual property (in this case the patents court would be the appropriate forum). In other cases, parties to a dispute are being encouraged more and more to resolve their differences through other avenues, such as arbitration and alternative dispute resolution (ADR). The relative merits of litigation against arbitration are also discussed.

Preliminary matters

The prospects for enforcing a judgment and costs is another matter which should be given careful consideration from the very outset of a case. Plaintiffs frequently regard an impecunious defendant as a deficiency in the law, which is, of course, erroneous. Nevertheless, if the commercial viability of litigation is dubious, it is far better to warn a client before he embarks on an expensive claim with little or no prospect of recovering his investment (let alone any return for it). In every case a client should be told that once he climbs onto the litigation "merry-go-round" it can be difficult to jump off before the ride stops. If a plaintiff is going to commence proceedings he should be prepared to see them through to the bitter end if necessary. Clients sometimes misconstrue this sage advice as a lack of confidence in their case, but that should not deter the lawyer from giving it. If the client has the benefit of legal aid, a full explanation of the workings of the statutory charge should be provided to him in writing. Similarly, the costs implications of the other party or parties being legally-aided should be considered and clearly explained.

As a general observation, it is a curious historical feature of the way in which litigation is conducted that counsel's advice on evidence is generally not sought at the outset of a claim. In fact, it is often the last request to be made of counsel which is sometimes several years after the initial advice was sought. Accordingly, if counsel's initial instructions are limited to advice on the merits of the case, the task of identifying and then gathering the raw material to substantiate the claim will fall on the shoulders of the solicitor. The other decision which the solicitor will have to make is whether to instruct counsel to settle the required pleadings. Like so many other things this is a question of judgment, and involves taking account of a number of factors, including the complexity of the claim, its value, the depth of the client's pockets, and the drafting expertise of the solicitor. It is easy to commence proceedings, but it is often difficult to bring them to a successful conclusion, especially where the case has not been adequately pleaded. Having to amend pleadings can often be a very expensive exercise, especially as a case reaches its conclusion. Indeed, if the amendment completely recasts a claim, a defendant may be entitled to all the costs of the action to the date of the amendment (see *Beoco Ltd* v *Alfa Laval Co Ltd* [1995] QB 137).

Evidence

The first step in any case is to obtain a full proof of evidence from the client, which will form the basis of a witness statement to be used in any subsequent proceedings. In that regard, as in so many others, a sports-related claim is no different from any other. If witnesses are identified whose evidence might be capable of assisting the client's case, efforts should be made to obtain statements from them. There are several very good reasons why statements should be as contemporaneous to the event as possible. The first and obvious reason is that memories fade, and if a case is likely to turn on the recollections of the parties, as opposed to documentary evidence, delaying in taking statements could be negligent. Furthermore, if all other things are equal, contemporaneous statements may carry more weight with the court than statements which were prepared months or even years after the event. If the recollections of a witness are derived from a contemporaneous record such as a diary, that is clearly a material piece of evidence which should be relied upon. It is often forgotten that there is no property in a witness. Accordingly, a witness who is initially identified as being supportive of a client's case, but who is not then approached to provide a statement, may end up giving evidence for the other side.

Physical evidence should also be gathered as quickly as possible, especially where there is a risk that it might be damaged, disposed of, or altered in any way. For example, a client might complain that he injured his leg during a football match as a consequence of tripping on a depression in the pitch which had not been filled in properly following maintenance works. The first task should be to photograph and measure the offending area, *not* to write a letter before action to the local council responsible for the maintenance of the pitch. The result such a letter is likely to achieve is the carrying out of remedial works, thereby obliterating crucial evidence, and a letter in reply containing a terse denial of liability from a hard-nosed insurance company. In certain instances it may be necessary to apply for a mandatory injunction, for example where a client alleges that he injured himself by slipping on the floor of a sports hall which is about to be demolished, or to restrain a professional sportsmen, who is contractually bound to play for one club, from playing for another. An application for pre-action discovery may need to be considered in addition to, or instead of, an application for an injunction (see RSC Ord 24, r 7(A), applied to the county court by CCR Ord 13, r 7(1)(g)).

In a personal injury claim arising out of a "dirty tackle", the following additional inquiries should be undertaken.

- If the incident was reported to the police, copies of the statements taken as part of any enquiry should be obtained. Such statements will invariably be taken contemporaneously with the incident and will hopefully provide reliable corroborative evidence.
- Statements should be obtained from the match officials. If the referee saw the incident what action did he take (*e.g.* did he award a free-kick or a penalty and did he book or send off the alleged assailant?). If the referee prepared a match report, this should be requested. So-called "off the ball" incidents frequently go unnoticed by officials who are concentrating on the play itself. If all three officials missed an alleged assault this may lend weight to the contention that it was deliberately inflicted whilst everyone else was looking the other way.
- If the client received hospital treatment, copies of any casualty records should be obtained. They may reveal tell-tale signs of a deliberately, or negligently, inflicted injury, such as stud marks.
- Film or video footage of the incident if available should be obtained, notwithstanding the doubt which Drake J cast on the usefulness of such evidence after seeing a video replayed countless times in the *Elliot* case (see Chapter 5).
- It may also be a good idea to obtain the defendant's disciplinary record This could involve making a request to the sporting body in question and, potentially, an application for discovery against a non-party if the request is refused (see RSC Ord 24, r 7A and CCR Ord 13, r 7(1)(g)). Inspection of property in such cases is governed by RSC Order 29, rule 7A.

Copies of the relevant codes, rules and laws should also be obtained. For example, FINA and the Amateur Swimming Association (ASA) both issue recommendations on the safe height of diving boards depending on the depth of swimming pools. Similar guidance is provided in relation to many other sports, including skiing and rugby union.

Expert evidence

Medical evidence

At the initial stages it is important to consider whether expert evidence is required and, if so, whom to instruct. In a personal injury case the rules provide that a claim must be accompanied by a medical report unless leave has been obtained to commence proceedings without such a report (see CCR Ord 6, r 1(5)(a)). Too many medical reports are prepared without the benefit of the consultant or doctor having sight of the plaintiff's medical and hospital records. Similarly, there are many consultants and doctors who are prepared to write a report, but who have an inadequate grasp of medico-legal issues. A medical expert should be chosen who understands critical legal issues such as causation and who can express his opinion in terms of legal certainty (*e.g.* "on a balance of probabilities" or "a high degree of certainty", as appropriate). If he specialises in sports injuries, this is even better. Another criticism which is sometimes levelled by judges is that medical reports suffer from an excess of specialist terminology which makes them difficult to understand.

Non-medical expert evidence

In the sporting context, non-medical experts might include the manufacturer of equipment, professional sportsmen, and respected sports officials. However, the *Elliot* case (above) highlights the dangers of calling an array of such witnesses who can be vulnerable under cross-examination and may end up contradicting one another. The need to involve an expert at an early stage will be all the more pressing if "at risk" physical evidence needs to be examined by him. Another implication of instructing an expert after the pleadings have been settled is that the client's pleaded case might not accurately reflect the expert's opinion. All too often the pressure of time-limits dictates that there is insufficient time to gather the necessary evidence before proceedings have to be issued. In those circumstances the prospect of having to amend at a later stage may have to be accepted, but whenever the need to do so can be avoided it should be.

Forum – High Court or county court?

In the absence of a negotiated settlement prior to the need to commence proceedings, the next decision is in which forum the claim should be brought. If a contract or convention is involved, it may specify the method for resolving the dispute and the state law to be applied. Alternatively, the parties may consent to the matter being dealt with by way of arbitration, or one of the methods of alternative dispute resolution (discussed in Chapter 10). Otherwise, claims will be litigated in the traditional way, namely by way of ordinary action either in the High Court or county court. Since the introduction of the High Court and County Courts Jurisdiction Order 1991 (SI 1991/724), the jurisdiction of the two courts has effectively been the same, the county court enjoying unlimited jurisdiction in tort and contract matters. Rule 7 of the Order provides that any action valued at less than £25,000 shall be tried in the county court, with actions valued at £50,000 to be tried in the High Court unless:

- an action valued at £25,000 or less is commenced in the High Court, and the High Court considers the matter to be one of substance or complexity (to be determined in accordance with criteria laid down in the Order);
- an action valued at £50,000 or more is commenced in the county court, and the county court does not consider the matter to be one of substance or complexity when judged against the same criteria.

If proceedings in a personal injury action are commenced in the High Court, the writ should be endorsed with a certificate to the effect that the estimated value of the claim is £50,000 or more (r 5 of the Order). The value of an action is the amount which the plaintiff reasonably expects to recover by way of damages and/or other money's worth, but excludes interest and costs. The ultimate sanction for an error in jurisdiction is for the High Court to exercise its discretion in favour of striking the claim out (see *Restick* v *Crickmore* [1994] 1 WLR 420), although such a Draconian step is only likely to occur where it is plain that the action should have been commenced in the county court, and the failure to do so was not due to a bona fide mistake. In any other case, the court is likely to transfer the case to the county court, subject to any costs implications. It can be seen, therefore, that if High Court proceedings in a personal injury claim are contemplated the significance of making an accurate assessment of the value of the claim cannot be underestimated.

No such requirement exists in relation to contractual claims, although litigating an uncomplicated contractual dispute in the High Court where the claim is worth less than £50,000 runs the risk that costs will only be allowed on the county court scale. An unsuccessful interlocutory application in such a case will almost certainly lead to its transfer to a suitable county court. Indeed, the High Court has power, of its own motion, to transfer actions valued at less than £50,000. Some consider that interlocutory matters such as applications for summary judgment will be dealt with more robustly by a Master than a district judge, although one suspects that the evidence to support that notion is purely anecdotal. The other perceived benefit of issuing in the High Court is that a plaintiff has more control over the destiny of the proceedings than in the county court. However, that is probably a matter of personal preference. Ultimately, the transfer down of a case commenced in the High Court often means that the entire action will only be allowed on the county court scale.

In both the High Court and the county court the time for service is four months from the date of issue, or six months in the case of service outside the jurisdiction (see RSC Ord 6, r 8 and CCR Ord 7, r 20(1)). Delaying service should be avoided if possible, especially where proceedings have been commenced just before the limitation period was due to expire. Nevertheless, it may be necessary where, for example, the defendant cannot be served for some reason, or the plaintiff is awaiting further evidence without which he would not be able to sustain his claim.

Litigate or arbitrate?

The decision whether to litigate or submit to arbitration will, in many small non-personal injury claims, automatically be made for the parties by virtue of the value of the claim (see CCR Ord 19, r 7). On the other hand, if both parties consent there is nothing to prevent a claim being referred to arbitration even where it does not fall to be automatically referred. Arbitration proceedings are intended to be informal, and the parties are encouraged to represent themselves, where possible. The strict rules of evidence do not apply in arbitrations, but it is a rare case where the extra latitude given to the court makes any real difference to the outcome. In cases where the parties have a choice, perhaps the most important consideration in deciding whether to arbitrate is that of costs, the normal rule being that each side bears its own costs irrespective of the outcome. That may be of benefit to a plaintiff whose prospects of success are by no means certain, and/or where the likely costs of pursuing the claim will be disproportionate to the amount at issue. Costs can be awarded against a party, but only if that party is shown to have acted unreasonably. In practice, a small claims hearing closely resembles a case which proceeds by way of ordinary action, although the former invariably take place in chambers, with the parties seated around a table. In a bid to save costs, a party to an arbitration may be represented at the hearing itself by a lay representative, rather than a lawyer, and there is nothing to stop such a third party from giving *ad hoc* advice as the claim progresses.

Limitation

By now it should be apparent that anyone who holds themselves out as a specialist in sports-related law will have to master a very broad knowledge. The more likely scenario is a working knowledge of the various areas of law which have been discussed. At the risk of stating the obvious, the essential limitation periods to remember are:

- in cases where personal injury has occurred due to the alleged negligence, nuisance or breach of duty of the defendant, the primary limitation period is three years from the date of the accident alleged to have caused the injury complained of, or from the date of knowledge that the injury was significant, whichever is later (s 11 of the Limitation Act 1980);
- where trespass to the person is alleged, the limitation period is six years from the date of the alleged assault (see *Stubbings v Webb* [1993] AC 498 which is authority for the proposition that injuries inflicted in a deliberate assault are outside the scope of s 11 of the 1980 Act and are therefore not covered by s 33); and
- in cases which involve an alleged breach of contract, the limitation period is six years from the date of the alleged breach (s 5).

The second limitation period may seem unfamiliar. Prior to *Stubbings* assaults or batteries were regarded as torts subject to a six-year limitation period provided for by section 2 of the 1980 Act. However, the point has already been made that a personal injury claim alleging trespass to the person will invariably plead negligence in the alternative, in which case proceedings will have to be brought within three years of the act complained of. Unless there is good reason for doing so, the issue of proceedings should not be delayed until the very end of the limitation period, as to do so may reflect badly on a plaintiff.

Infants and other persons under a legal disability

Claims are often made on behalf of minors; and a good working knowledge of the law applicable to persons who are deemed to be under a legal disability is also essential. The classes of person who do not have full legal capacity include infants (*i.e.* those under the age of 18) and patients (who are incapable, by reason of mental disorder, from managing and administering their property and affairs). An infant's presumed disability continues until he acquires his majority at the age of 18 and, conceivably, he could wait until just before his 21st birthday before suing for damages in respect of personal injuries caused by a defendant's negligence (see s 28(6) of the Limitation Act 1980). However, if the accident happened at a very tender age, refraining from suing for many years runs the inevitable risk that the claim will become stale, and the evidence in support of it will be weakened or lost. Each case will have to be judged on its own facts, but the best course will nearly always be to gather the evidence with speed and efficiency, and then sue if a negotiated settlement cannot be reached. Another point to watch out for is any potential conflict of interest between an infant and his proposed next friend. Typically, such a conflict arises where criticism is capable of attaching to a parent for his part in a child's accident. In such a case, it is better for someone unconnected with the accident to act as the child's next friend (a maternal grandmother for example). If a possible conflict is still perceived, application should be made to the Official Solicitor. Similar considerations apply to those under a mental disability.

Interlocutory matters

If counsel is instructed to settle particulars of claim he should also be asked to draft or approve the schedule of special damage, which technically forms part of the pleading. It is also good practice to instruct counsel to settle a reply and, if appropriate, a defence to counterclaim. At the interlocutory stage a plaintiff should consider the viability of making an application for summary judgment and/or an interim payment, if only to dismiss both options on the ground that they are unlikely to succeed. The procedure for making an application for summary judgement is set out in RSC Order 14, rule 9 and CCR Order 9, rule 14, but such an application should only be made in personal injury claims in the very clearest of cases (see *Rapley* v *P&O Ferries* (1991) *Independent*, 18 March, CA); it is also inappropriate where there is a complicated issue over the construction of documents (see *Balli Trading Ltd* v *Afalone Shipping Ltd* (1992) 136 Sol Jo 258, CA). At the risk of stating the obvious, a judgment will have to be made in each case based on the relative strengths and weaknesses of the plaintiff's case. When acting for a defendant the first thing to establish is whether the contents of the affidavit in support of an application for summary judgment complies with the procedural requirements of RSC Order 14, rules 1 and 2 (it is surprising how many do not). Any defects can be cured by further affidavit evidence (but not defects in the pleadings themselves), although at obvious risk as to costs. Another matter which is often inadequately dealt with in affidavits is the identification of the source or sources of hearsay evidence, which can be fatal to an application, especially if the master or district judge is a stickler for procedure.

For both sides to a dispute, a well-drafted and well-directed request for further and better particulars can explore and expose weaknesses in the other side's case. Interogatorries are also capable of being used to devastating effect, but their value is undermined by the argument that they compound, rather than clarify, the issues and it looks as if they will be eliminated as part of the Woolf proposals to streamline litigation.

A defendant should consider whether a payment into court should be made and, if so, how much to pay in. If it is to have the greatest possible effect, a payment in should be made as early in the proceedings as possible. Making a payment in shortly before trial might place the plaintiff at risk as to the costs of the trial, but he can still be confident that he will recover his costs of the action incurred prior to the payment in.

Defendants and their insurers still allow too much litigation to be conducted, for too long, at their expense. In some cases it will be difficult to assess the value of a claim, especially in a personal injury claim where the medical prognosis and/or the plaintiff's employment prospects are uncertain. There is little that a defendant can do in such situations, other than to evince an intention to the trial judge that there had always been a willingness to negotiate, which ought to be reflected in the costs order made. However, a *Calderbank* offer will not protect a defendant in costs where a payment into court can be made.

Preparation for trial

Witness statements

If the case is brought in the county court, the requirements of CCR Order 17, rule 11, or any bespoke directions which have been made, should be strictly adhered to, especially by a plaintiff. If the ramifications of *Rastin v British Steel* [1994] 1 WLR 733 and subsequent Court of Appeal decisions concerning automatic directions were considered by the legal profession to be punitive, the recent decision in *Beachley Property Services v Edgar* (1996) *The Times*, 18 July underlines the unforgiving way in which the Court of Appeal can interpret procedural rules. Shortly before the date set for trial in the latter case, the plaintiff applied for leave, pursuant to CCR Order 20, rule 12A, to adduce the evidence of three further witnesses at trial. The plaintiff's excuse for failing to comply with the directions made in the case was that there had been a change of personnel in the offices of its solicitors. The Court of Appeal regarded that as no excuse, and the application was emphatically dismissed.

The harshness of *Beachley* was ameliorated, to some extent, by the subsequent ruling of the Court of Appeal in *Letpak and others v Harris* (1996) *The Times*, 6 December. It is not easy to reconcile the two decisions, particularly the extent to which any prejudice the other party may have suffered is relevant. Perhaps the main distinction is that the further evidence in *Beachley* merely assisted the plaintiff's case, whereas in *Letpak* the plaintiff would have been unable to continue with its claim if the application to adduce further evidence had been refused. Following those two cases, the Court of Appeal gave 10 principles of general guidance to be applied when dealing with applications of this kind, in *Mortgage Corporation Ltd v Sandoes and others* (1996) *The Times*, 27 December. The clear message is those who miss deadlines for the exchange of witness statements, or do not serve all the evidence upon which they intend to rely at trial, do so at their peril.

The key point in *Beachley*, which survives both the *Letpak* and *Mortgage Corporation* cases, is that if the granting of leave to serve statements out of time would necessitate an adjournment of a trial, then it will be extremely difficult to persuade a judge to exercise his discretion to admit them. The policy which avoids that risk and which seems to find favour with the judges, is to give due warning that the mutual exchange of witness statements should take place by a certain date and to send the statements at the appointed time even if the other side say that it is not in a position to reciprocate. In the past, the argument against voluntary disclosure of witness statements has always been that it gives the other side the advantage of preparing its statements having had sight of the other party's statements (*i.e.* "I'll show you mine, if you show me yours", which is surely what "mutual exchange" was intended to achieve). The simple answer is now to take the *Beachley* point against an opponent who fails to disclose his statements on time. If there is a good reason why statements cannot be exchanged, or any other step taken, in accordance with the directions timetable, the remedy is to make an application to the court for an extension of the time for compliance.

On an allied, but slightly different point there may be good tactical reasons for voluntarily disclosing one's evidence from the very outset, primarily where the strength of the client's case is such that the other side is likely to capitulate. It is a bold but justifiable step to take in the right case. The new culture which has been imposed on civil litigation means that responsibility for ensuring that a claim is prosecuted efficiently towards a conclusion rests firmly with the plaintiff. It is not a valid excuse to blame a defendant for dragging his feet; such behaviour should be visited with applications for peremptory orders.

The contents of the statements themselves are no less important. Although the practice varies from court to court, most county court judges are prepared to allow supplementary questions to be asked in order to cover ground which is not included in a witness statement. However, depending on the importance of the additional evidence elicited in that manner, it is a safe bet that the other side will seek to capitalise on it. Additionally, there may be inconsistencies between a witness's statement and any oral evidence due usually to all-too brief statements or poor draftmanship, rather than a failure on the part of the witness to provide adequate instructions. If it is the latter, and the information later coaxed out of the witness by supplementary questions is significant, it begs the question: why was it not elicited when the statement was taken? The commercial court is far less forgiving than the county court when dealing with supplementary evidence and a good practice to adopt in every case is to assume that a statement will stand as the evidence-in-chief of the witness and that no further questions will be permitted.

Hearsay evidence

It may be necessary to serve a witness summons or subpoena in order to compel the attendance of a particular witness at court. This is also a prudent step to take where a witness has indicated his willingness to attend court but might, due to other commitments, be unable to do so (*e.g.* a busy consultant surgeon). If a case has to be adjourned due to the non-attendance of a crucial witness, the production of a witness summons or subpoena should eliminate any risk of a wasted costs order being made. If a witness is unable to attend, either on the date set for the hearing or at all, steps will need to be taken to ensure that his statement or report is received in evidence. The Civil Evidence Act 1995, which came into force on 31 January 1997, effectively sweeps away the hearsay provisions contained in Part I of the Civil Evidence Act 1968. In particular, the complicated requirements in relation to computer-generated evidence are consigned to the scrap heap. The requirement to serve notice of a party's intention to use hearsay evidence remains, but the procedure is more straightforward than previously and, just as under the former legislation, there is power to admit evidence where the formalities have not been complied with (although such a failure is a factor to consider when the court comes to consider costs). Under the new regime, it seems likely that most evidence will go in and the court will then simply have to decide how much weight should be attached to it.

Bundles

Trial bundles should be indexed and paginated, and preferably contained in a lever arch file, enabling documents to be inserted and taken out with ease. The next best option is a ring binder or, if there are only a very small number of documents, treasury tags. Binding the documents together with staples or sealing should be avoided at all costs. Bundles should be lodged with the court as early as possible and, in any event, not less than seven days before the trial is due to take place (see CCR Ord 17, r12(3)). The bundle should be arranged in sections, with the pleadings first, followed by any orders which may be relevant. The next section should comprise each side's witness statements and experts' reports (if any). The correspondence and other documents which it is intended to rely upon should then be set out in chronological order. If one bundle is likely to be cumbersome, it may be necessary to have two or more. On a related point, if agreement cannot be reached over the inclusion of certain documents, it is far better to include them in a second, self-contained bundle than for each side to lodge its own bundles. If the judge rules that certain documents are admissable, they can then be inserted at the appropriate place in the main bundle.

Chapter 12

Pleadings and Forms

Introduction

Since sports-related litigation covers such a broad spectrum, it is impossible to provide the reader with anything other than a brief sample of the types of pleadings and other documents which might be used in practice. In this final chapter, some examples are given of those forms which are most likely to be required, and it is hoped that they will provide at least some guidance. I deliberately avoid the use of the word "precedent" in case it is thought that the forms should be followed slavishly. There is no magic to settling pleadings in sports-related cases, but it may be necessary to consider whether any rules and regulations, statutory or otherwise, apply. For example, when dealing with an accident in a school games lesson, it may be a good idea to plead a failure on the part of the teacher to observe the guidance introduced to enable schools to determine the suitability of certain activities for particular age-groups (see Chapter 6). There may also be certain matters that need to be pleaded by virtue of a particular statute, or rules of court, such as a claim brought by dependants under the Fatal Accidents Act 1976.

Pleading style varies, but there are certain basic principles to which every practitioner should adhere. First, the essence of good pleading is an ability to communicate a client's case in a form which can easily be understood. The old adage "tell the story" still holds good, although there is often a thin dividing line between a recital of the facts and falling into the trap of pleading evidence. A good practice to adopt – and this applies both to plaintiffs and defendants – is to compartmentalise the other side's pleadings in order to identify, and then respond to, the issues raised. When responding to particulars, it is always preferable to adopt the same paragraph or subparagraph numbering as the pleading which are being responded to. This will make it easier for the parties and the court to reconcile the corresponding averments and traverses. Discrete paragraphs or sub-paragraphs should be used, if necessary, for making individual points, especially if there is a danger of the issues becoming lost under the weight of the facts. Lengthy paragraphs which recite the facts *ad nauseam*, or which advance a number of unrelated propositions, are difficult to plead to and difficult for the court to digest. Using two words when one will do should be avoided and colloquialisms should never be used in formal pleadings.

The examples I have chosen are representative of some of the key issues which have emerged during the course of this book, and include a claim for a further payment under a transfer contract (a variation on the theme in *Bournemouth and Boscombe Athletic Football Club Co Ltd* v *Manchester United Football Club Ltd* (1980) *The Times*, 21 May), a personal injury claim arising out of a "dirty tackle" in a football match, and an interlocutory application for a declaration that a disciplinary hearing breached the rules of natural justice (in the context of a private law action, *not* an application for judicial review). There are also a number of ancillary forms, including a letter before action, a witness statement and a notice of application, together with an accompanying affidavit (in practice, there would also, of course, be a writ). The form and substance of a Civil Evidence Act notice is unlikely to have any material differences irrespective of whether it is under the 1968 Act or the 1995 Act. A degree of humour has been injected where appropriate, and any resemblance the parties to, or issues involved in, the imaginary proceedings may have to present or past individuals or bodies is purely coincidental.

Example 1

Letter before action for breach of contract for transfer of footballer; allegation that player not given a reasonable opportunity to play and score goals which would give rise to further payment(s) under the contract

To the defendant

Dear Sirs,

We act for Sudbury Strollers from whom you will recall you purchased Peter Punter at the beginning of the 1996/97 season for a basic transfer fee of £500,000. It was a condition of the transfer agreement (by clause 12(a)) that if Mr Punter scored 20 goals in his first season with you, a further £100,000 would become payable to our Client, and a further £5,000 for each subsequent goal.

Our Client informs us that Punter scored 15 goals in the first 20 games of the season, and was in your first team's starting line-up for each match. Since then, he has only started in five first team games in 25 matches and has been named as a substitute in 10 other games. When he was named as a substitute, Punter only came on for the last 10 minutes in two matches, and in the remaining 10 matches he did not even make the substitutes' bench. So far as our Client is aware, Punter has been free of injury all season and could have played in every single match, if selected.

We would refer you to clause 12(b) of the transfer contract which expressly provides that Punter would be given a reasonable opportunity to play for your first team. It is self-evident from the above facts that you have not afforded him that opportunity and, as a consequence, he has not been able to score the goals which would have taken him over the 20-goal threshold, thereby entitling our Client to a further sum from you. Indeed, had Punter been in the starting line-up for the majority of the matches, and repeated his form of the first 20 games, it is likely that he would have scored over 30 goals over the course of the season.

Accordingly, we are instructed by our Client to pursue you for an additional sum under the above-mentioned terms of the contract. Unless we receive satisfactory settlement proposals from you within the next 14 days, we intend to issue proceedings on behalf of our Client in the Colchester County Court without further recourse to you.

Yours faithfully,

.

Example 2

Particulars of claim referred to in Example 1

Case No CO123456

IN THE COLCHESTER COUNTY COURT

BETWEEN

SUDBURY STROLLERS

Plaintiff

and

TOPDOG UNITED

Defendant

PARTICULARS OF CLAIM

1. By a written agreement dated 1 August 1996 (the Agreement), the Plaintiff agreed to sell, and the Defendant agreed to buy, property belonging to the Plaintiff, namely the footballer Sid Punter for a basic transfer fee of £500,000.

2. The following were express terms of the Agreement:

   (i) by clause 12(a) thereof, that if the said Sid Punter scored 20 goals for the Defendant's first team in the 1996/97 football season, the sum of £50,000 would immediately become due and payable to the Plaintiff, and an additional sum of £5,000 for each subsequent goal which the Plaintiff scored; and
   (ii) by clause 12(b) thereof, that Sid Punter would be given a reasonable opportunity to play for the Defendant's first team during the course of the 1996/97 football season.

3. In breach of the express term referred to at paragraph 2(ii) herein, Sid Punter was not given a reasonable opportunity to play in the Defendant's first team during the course of the 1996/97 football season.

PARTICULARS

The Defendant's first team played a total of 45 matches during the course of the season. Sid Punter was in the starting line-up for the first 20 games and scored a total of 15 goals. In the remaining 25 games, he only made the starting line-up on five occasions. He was named as a substitute in 10 other games, but only came on to play for the last 10 minutes in two matches. He did not make the substitutes' bench in the remaining 10 matches. Sid Punter did not suffer any injuries during the course of the season and was fit to play in every game, if selected.

4.   By reason of the Defendant's said breach of contract the Plaintiff has suffered loss and damage.

PARTICULARS OF DAMAGE

The Plaintiff's case is that if Sid Punter had been given a reasonable opportunity to play for the Defendant's first team, it is highly probable that he would have scored at least 20 goals over the course of the said season. Based on his goal-scoring form in the first 20 matches, it is reasonable to assume that Sid Punter would have scored in the region of 30 goals had he been afforded a reasonable opportunity to play, thereby entitling the Plaintiff to receive a further payment under clause 12(a) of the agreement. The Plaintiff is unable to quantify the precise number of goals which Sid Punter would have scored had he been given a reasonable opportunity to play for the Defendant's first team and therefore claims general damages to be assessed.

5.   Further, the Plaintiff is entitled to interest pursuant to section 69 of the County Courts Act 1984 on the amount found to be due to the Plaintiff at such rate and for such period as the Court thinks fit.

AND the Plaintiff claims:

(1) Damages, which exceed £10,000, to be assessed.
(2) The aforesaid interest pursuant to statute to be assessed.

Signed

Dated *etc*

Example 3

Defence to claim in Example 2: defendant acted in good faith; reliance on implied term that player would be available for selection; allegation of misconduct

Case No CO123456

IN THE COLCHESTER COUNTY COURT

BETWEEN

SUDBURY STROLLERS

Plaintiff

and

TOPDOG UNITED

Defendant

DEFENCE

1. Paragraphs 1 and 2 are admitted.

2. The express terms of the contract set out at paragraph 2 of the particulars of claim were subject to an implied term that Sid Punter would not, either by his misconduct on or off the field, or by any other means, do anything to prevent him from being selected to play for the Defendant's first team and/or which might justify those responsible for picking the said first team in not selecting Sid Punter.

3. It is admitted that Sid Punter was dropped from the Defendant's first team after playing in the first 20 games of the 1996/97 season and averred that the Defendant acted reasonably and in good faith in doing so.

PARTICULARS

The Defendant will rely on the following facts and matters at trial:

(i) Following the Premier League match between the Defendant and Melchester City on 1 December 1996, Sid Punter swore at, and physically assaulted, Melchester City supporters as a consequence of which he was banned from playing for two games by the Football Association. That ban was subsequently extended to five games when Sid Punter appeared on *Match of the Day* and announced that the FA's Disciplinary Committee were "a bunch of oafs".

(ii) Whilst he was serving his ban, the Plaintiff's place in the team was taken by Alan Sheerhell who scored eight goals in five games. When Sid Punter was advised by the Defendant's coach, Joe Carcoat, that he would have to fight his way back into the first team, Sid Punter told Joe Carcoat that he (Carcoat) knew more about cheap champagne than he did about football. Sid Punter then failed to attend the next 15 training sessions and was placed on the transfer list by the Defendant after refusing to pay a £2,000 club fine.

4. Further or alternatively, the Defendant relies on the implied term referred to at paragraph 2 herein and avers that Sid Punter precluded himself from selection for the Defendant's first team by his aforesaid ban and misconduct.

5. In the premises, it is denied that the Defendant is in breach of contract, whether as alleged at paragraph 3 of the particulars of claim or at all. The Plaintiff's alleged entitlement to statutory interest is also denied.

Signed

Served *etc*

Example 4

Statement of claim: professional footballer injured by tackle which allegedly amounted to an assault; negligence pleaded in the alternative. Proceedings brought against both the player responsible for the tackle and his club; claim worth in excess of £50,000

1997 S No 305

IN THE HIGH COURT OF JUSTICE
QUEEN'S BENCH DIVISION

BETWEEN

GARY SPINNAKER

Plaintiff

and

(1) NOBBY "BONECRUSHER" SMITH
(2) CARSHALTON CASUALS

Defendants

STATEMENT OF CLAIM

1. At all material times:

    (i) the Plaintiff was a professional footballer, playing for Melchester Rovers in the Football Association Premier League; and

    (ii) the First Defendant was employed by the Second Defendant as a professional footballer, and also played in the said Premier League.

2. On 1 January 1996 the Plaintiff was playing in a Premier League match for Melchester Rovers against the Second Defendant at the Second Defendant's Grim Valley ground in Croydon, Surrey. The First Defendant was playing for the Second Defendant in the said match in the course of his said employment. Shortly before half-time, the Plaintiff was chasing a ball in the middle of the field when he was tackled from behind by the First Defendant, striking the Plaintiff on his right knee and causing him to suffer personal injury and loss and damage hereinafter referred to.

3. When he made the said tackle, the First Defendant intended to cause the Plaintiff bodily injury, alternatively the First Defendant

was reckless as to whether he would cause the Plaintiff such injury. The Plaintiff will rely, *inter alia*, on the First Defendant's statement, made prior to the said match, that he "would do Spinnaker", together with the nature and extent of the Plaintiff's injury, as evidence of the First Defendant's intention to injure the Plaintiff.

4. Further or alternatively, the Plaintiff's injury, loss and damage was caused by the negligence of the First Defendant for which the Second Defendant is vicariously liable as his employer.

PARTICULARS OF NEGLIGENCE

(i)   Lunging at the Plaintiff from a distance of some 10 feet, at speed, and with both feet off the ground, a so-called two-footed tackle which was dangerous and likely to cause the Plaintiff injury.

(ii) Tackling the Plaintiff from behind, contrary to Law 12 of the Rules of Association Football and FIFA Regulations.

(iii) Failing to have any or any adequate regard for the Plaintiff's safety.

5. By reason of the aforesaid facts and matters the Plaintiff has suffered personal injury and sustained loss and damage.

PARTICULARS OF INJURY

Following the incident, the Plaintiff was taken to hospital where a ruptured cruciate ligament was diagnosed. His right leg was initially placed in a full-length plaster and he subsequently underwent three separate operations under general anaesthetic to replace the torn ligament with an artificial one. He then underwent nine months of intensive physiotherapy and eventually resumed light training on 1 April 1997, 15 months after sustaining the injury. During that period he was unable to play football and lost his place in both his club and national sides. He has made a good recovery from his injury but it is unlikely that he will play at international level again. He has also been left with extensive and permanent residual scarring to the knee.

A copy of the medical report of Professor Pat Pending FRCS, Consultant Orthopaedic Surgeon, dated 20 March 1997, is annexed hereto.

PARTICULARS OF SPECIAL DAMAGE

A schedule is annexed hereto [*in addition to the usual heads of special damage, items of loss in a case such as this might include loss of win bonuses, appearance monies etc. It may be necessary to plead some, or all, of any anticipated financial benefits as the loss of a chance, in the alternative to an actual loss*].

6. Further, the Plaintiff is entitled to and claims interest pursuant to section 35A of the Supreme Court Act 1981 on the amount found to be due to him at such rate and for such period as the Court thinks fit.

AND the Plaintiff claims:

(1) Damages which exceed £50,000.
(2) The aforesaid interest pursuant to statute to be assessed.

Signed

Dated *etc*

Example 5

Defence of the first defendant to claim in Example 4: defence that tackle was fair and reasonable; plea of volenti; allegation of contributory negligence

1997 S No 305

IN THE HIGH COURT OF JUSTICE
QUEEN'S BENCH DIVISION

BETWEEN

GARY SPINNAKER

Plaintiff

and

(1) NOBBY "BONECRUSHER" SMITH
(2) CARSHALTON CASUALS

Defendants

DEFENCE OF THE FIRST DEFENDANT

---

1. Paragraph 1 of the Statement of Claim is admitted.

2. It is admitted that:

    (i)   the Plaintiff suffered some injury (the nature and extent of which is not admitted) in a tackle with the First Defendant during a Premier League match on 1 January 1996 at the Second Defendant's ground; and
    (ii) immediately prior to the collision between them, the Plaintiff and the First Defendant were both chasing the ball which, it is averred, the First Defendant had a reasonable chance of winning fairly;
    (iii) in the course of the said tackle, the Plaintiff was accidentally caught on the right knee by the First Defendant's right boot.

    And in the premises, it is averred that any injury which the Plaintiff may prove to have sustained occurred accidentally as the First Defendant won the ball with a fair and reasonable tackle. The First Defendant will rely, *inter alia*, on the fact that the match referee did not award any foul, or take any action, against the First Defendant arising out of the said incident.

3. Further or alternatively, the Plaintiff will rely on the maxim volenti non fit injuria and contend that the Plaintiff impliedly consented to the risk of accidental injury when he played in the said match. Save as aforesaid, paragraph 2 the Statement of Claim is not admitted and paragraph 3 thereof is denied.

4. Further or alternatively, the Plaintiff's injury was caused wholly by, or was contributed to by, the negligence of the Plaintiff in failing properly to commit himself to the said tackle and/or hesitating as he challenged for the ball with the First Defendant, thereby exposing himself to the risk of injury.

5. By reason of the aforesaid facts and matters, the First Defendant denies that he is liable to the Plaintiff, whether as alleged or at all.

6. Save that it is admitted that the Plaintiff suffered some injury when he collided with the First Defendant, no admissions are made as to the nature or extent thereof, or as to the alleged loss and damage claimed, liability for which is, in any event, denied. The Plaintiff's alleged entitlement to statutory interest is also denied.

Signed

Served *etc*

Example 6

Defence of the second defendant to claim in Example 4: adopting the defence of the first defendant and denying vicarious liability in the event that the first defendant, as its employee, is found to have assaulted the plaintiff

1997 S No 305

IN THE HIGH COURT OF JUSTICE
QUEEN'S BENCH DIVISION

BETWEEN

GARY SPINNAKER

Plaintiff

and

(1) NOBBY "BONECRUSHER" SMITH
(2) CARSHALTON CASUALS

Defendants

DEFENCE OF THE SECOND DEFENDANT

1. Save as hereinafter appears, the Second Defendant adopts the Defence of the First Defendant as if the same were set out and repeated herein.

2. If, which is denied, the First Defendant is found to have assaulted the Plaintiff during the said match, whether as alleged or at all, the Second Defendant will aver that the First Defendant acted outside the scope of the express and/or implied terms of his contract of employment at the material time and that the Second Defendant is not liable to the Plaintiff for any injury, loss or damage which he may have suffered as a consequence (which injury, loss and damage is not admitted in any event).

3. In the premises, it is denied that the Second Defendant is liable to the Plaintiff whether as alleged or at all.

Signed

Served *etc*

Example 7

Witness statement of the plaintiff in support of claim in Example 4

1997 S No 305

IN THE HIGH COURT OF JUSTICE
QUEEN'S BENCH DIVISION

BETWEEN

GARY SPINNAKER

Plaintiff

and

(1) NOBBY "BONECRUSHER" SMITH
(2) CARSHALTON CASUALS

Defendants

WITNESS STATEMENT OF THE PLAINTIFF

I, Gary Spinnaker, of 12 Kings Road, Chelsea, London, will say as follows:

1. I am the Plaintiff in these proceedings. I am a professional footballer and at the beginning of the 1995/96 season was signed by Melchester Rovers for a then world record fee of £15 million. On 1 January 1996 Melchester played in a Premier League match against Carshalton Casuals at the Casuals' Grim Valley ground. There had been an undercurrent of bad feeling between the two sides for some time, particularly after Melchester had beaten Carshalton in the final of the Drainex Cleaning Fluid Cup Final in 1994. Three of Carshalton's players were sent off in that game, including the First Defendant. I did not take part in that game, but did play in the League match which took place between the two sides on 3 September 1995 at Melchester's ground. It was an acrimonious game, to say the least, following which the First Defendant went on television claiming that Melchester were "a bunch of fairies" and that he would "sort Spinnaker out" in the return fixture. He was disciplined by the FA for those comments but, as far as I am aware, his Club (the Second Defendant) took no action against him.

2. Feelings were therefore running high for the game on 1 January 1996 which had not been helped by all the media attention, as both sides were vying for the League title. The first half was a scrappy affair and was littered with many fouls, the vast majority of which were committed by Carshalton players. In fact, the Defendant was booked by the referee for a late challenge on my Brazilian striking partner, Edson de Oliviera (Olly). My injury occurred in the following way. It was approaching half-time and the ball ran loose in the centre circle where I was positioned. The ball was approaching from my left and I only had to adjust myself slightly in order to intercept it. Then, out of the corner of my eye, I noticed the Defendant running towards the ball from behind me, and to my left. He was some way away from me, approximately 30 feet and, although he was running at speed, I had no doubt that I would get the ball before him.

3. However, as I went to control the ball, the Defendant lunged at me from the edge of the centre circle with both feet off the ground, a distance of about 10 feet. He flew through the air, with a two-footed tackle, and there was nothing I could do to avoid him. The Defendant caught me with both feet on the back of my right leg, just below the knee joint. I took his full weight and as my knee buckled I felt something snap inside the joint. I knew straight away that I had seriously damaged my knee; the pain was excruciating. A number of players from both sides rushed towards me, as well as the Referee whom I saw separating a number of opposing players. After he had separated the ensuing melee, the Referee was obviously concerned for my welfare and I believe that he was more concerned with ensuring that I received treatment than considering whether to take action against the Defendant.

4. The Defendant has a well-publicised disciplinary record. He has been sent off 15 times during his career and been booked over 50 times. He has also been censured by the FA on several occasions for comments to the press, including those preceeding the match in which I was injured, and to which I have already referred. By contrast, I have never been booked in my 12-year professional career, let alone sent-off. It is suggested that my injury was caused because I was not fully committed to the challenge, or because I hesitated as I went in for the ball. As I have already stated, there was no doubt in my mind that I would comfortably

win the ball and to describe it as a 50-50 ball is totally incorrect. If I did momentarily hesitate (and I do not admit that I did), it would only have been in sheer disbelief that the Defendant would commit such a wild and reckless tackle. Video footage of the game will, I believe, bear that out.

5. Following the incident, I was immediately taken to hospital where a ruptured anterior cruciate ligament was diagnosed. I have undergone three operations under general anaesthetic, the first of which involved the removal of the damaged ligament which was sheared in two. A month later, an operation was performed to replace the ligament with an artificial one and I subsequently suffered an infection in the joint, hence the need for further surgery. The treatment of my injuries is set out in detail in the medical reports which have been commissioned on my behalf. At one stage, the Consultant Surgeon responsible for my treatment warned me that I might not play again. That warning spurred me on and I eventually resumed training on 1 April 1997 and have recently won my place back in the Melchester side. However, during the 15 months I was out of action, the team won the Premier League and then triumphed in the European Champions League. Had I been a part of the team, I would have been entitled to win bonuses totalling £150,000.

6. Although I have made a satisfactory recovery, there is now a limit to my physical capabilities which, I believe, will prevent me from ever playing football at international level again. Furthermore, while I may be able to continue playing at Premier League level for two or three more seasons, I will probably have to drop down a division a lot sooner than I would have done. I am currently earning £250,000 a year and my contract is due to expire at the end of the 1997/98 season. Had it not been for my injury, I would have anticipated renewing my contract with Melchester for a further three years. There is now a considerable doubt whether I will be offered a new contract. At current rates, I believe that I could command a salary of no more than £50,000 a year in the first division. I also earned, on average, £25,000 per annum in international appearance fees which I am likely to lose. I also believe that my sponsorship deals, currently worth £200,000 per annum, may be adversely affected if I were to stop playing Premier League football.

7. I confirm that the above statement represents a true and accurate record of the facts.

Signed ....

Dated ....

Example 8

County court claim by minor against education authority for injuries caused by teacher's failure to provide adequate training or instruction in how to use trampoline, and/or for failing properly to supervise physical education lesson at school; claim for provisional damages

Case No 180572

IN THE OXFORD COUNTY COURT

BETWEEN

SARAH JONES
(a minor who sues by her mother
and next friend, Susan Jones)

Plaintiff

and

MIDSHIRE COUNTY COUNCIL

Defendant

PARTICULARS OF CLAIM

1. The Plaintiff is and was at all material times a minor, her date of birth being 18 May 1985, and brings this claim by her mother and next friend, Susan Jones.

2. At all material times:

    (i)   the Defendant is and was the education authority responsible for the management and control of the Low Wycombe School for Girls, Low Wycombe, Buckinghamshire (the School), its teachers and staff; and
    (ii) the Plaintiff was a pupil at the School.

3. On 11 June 1996 the Plaintiff, in common with approximately 30 other pupils, was participating in a physical education lesson which took place in the gymnasium of the School. The Plaintiff had the choice of taking part in three separate activities and elected to do trampolining, an exercise which she had never done before. The Plaintiff was in a group of 10 pupils and when her turn came to use the trampoline she was jumping on the same

when she lost her balance and fell off the trampoline onto the hard surface of the gymnasium floor, suffering a serious fracture of her pelvis.

4.   The said accident was caused by the negligence of the Defendant, its servants or agents.

PARTICULARS OF NEGLIGENCE

(i)   Failing to give the Plaintiff any adequate training or instruction in how to use the trampoline safely when the teacher responsible for the lesson knew that the Plaintiff had never previously used a trampoline. The Plaintiff's case is that the teacher spent no more than two minutes instructing her group before leaving them to oversee another activity.

(ii)   Failing to have any, or any adequate, regard to the concepts of Programmes of Study or End of Key Stage Statements and, in particular, failing to assess the level of risk associated with 12-year-olds participating in trampolining activity and/or to minimise the risk of injury to the Plaintiff.

(iii) Failing to monitor and/or exercise any, or any adequate, supervision over the said trampolining activity in which the Plaintiff was participating.

(iv)   Failing to provide an adequate number of staff to supervise the said lesson.

(v)   Failing, in all the circumstances, to exercise a reasonable level of care for the Plaintiff's safety.

5.   By reason of the aforesaid facts and matters the Plaintiff suffered personal injury and sustained loss and damage.

PARTICULARS OF INJURY

Pain, suffering and loss of amenity already caused

[*A summary of the injuries in respect of which immediate damages are sought*]

A copy of the medical report of Dr David Owen FRCS, dated 3 March 1997, is annexed hereto. The Plaintiff reserves the right to serve further medical evidence in due course.

Risk of deterioration

The particulars of injury and claim for special damages and future loss do not take into account the chance that at some definite or indefinite time in the future the Plaintiff may, as a result of the Defendant's negligence, develop a serious deterioration in her physical condition, namely [*then go on to specify the contingency. In this case, for example, it might be*: a 50% risk of major hip reconstruction surgery, and a 10% risk that she will be totally disabled from the waist down, by the age of 30].

In the event of an award of provisional damages being refused, the Plaintiff will contend that there is a significant risk of further disability occurring during her lifetime. In that event, the Plaintiff will require major hip reconstruction surgery. In addition to the cost of such surgery, the Plaintiff will suffer further pain, suffering and loss of amenity. It is anticipated that she will require six months off school, college or work (as the case may be), in order to convalesce and rehabilitate.

PARTICULARS OF SPECIAL DAMAGE

A schedule of special damage and future loss is annexed hereto. The schedule does not take into account the further consequential losses which the Plaintiff would suffer if she should, at some time in the future, become disabled and wheelchair-bound. At today's values, the cost of surgery and aftercare is estimated at £250,000. Additionally, the Plaintiff would suffer a significant handicap in the labour market and/or loss of earning capacity.

6. Further, the Plaintiff is entitled to and claims interest pursuant to section 69 of the County Courts Act 1984 on the amount found to be due to her at such rate and for such period as the Court thinks fit.

AND the Plaintiff claims:

(1) Damages on the assumption that the Plaintiff will not, at a future date, as a result of the act or omission giving rise to the cause of action, develop the following serious deterioration in her

physical condition, namely a 50% risk that she will require major hip reconstruction surgery, and a 10% risk that she will be disabled from the waist down, by the age of 30.

(2) An order for the award of provisional damages under section 32A of the Supreme Court Act 1981 that if, at a future date, the Plaintiff developed such a condition she shall be entitled to apply for further damages.

(3) The aforesaid statutory interest to be assessed.

Signed

Dated *etc*

Example 9

Defence to claim in Example 8: adequate instruction given to pupils for limited scope of activity; disobedience of specific instruction; two pupils using trampoline at the same time; contributory negligence; denial that case qualifies for a provisional damage award

Case No 180572

IN THE OXFORD COUNTY COURT

BETWEEN

SARAH JONES
(a minor who sues by her mother
and next friend, Susan Jones)

Plaintiff

and

MIDSHIRE COUNTY COUNCIL

Defendant

DEFENCE

---

1. Paragraphs 1 and 2 of the particulars of claim are admitted.

2. Insofar as paragraph 3 of the particulars of claim purports to aver that the Plaintiff was using the trampoline unaccompanied when she fell from the same, it is denied.

3. Negligence, whether as alleged in paragraph 4 of the particulars of claim or otherwise is denied.

4. Without prejudice to the generality of the foregoing, the Defendant avers that the instruction of the Plaintiff's group lasted approximately 15 minutes, during which time the teacher in control of the class instructed the said group in basic jumping and safety techniques. The teacher then went to deal with another group and gave the Plaintiff's group a specific verbal instruction that they were to take turns in bouncing lightly on the trampoline and that they should not attempt to jump to any height.

5. The accident was caused or materially contributed to by the negligence of the Plaintiff.

PARTICULARS OF NEGLIGENCE

(i) Disobeying and/or ignoring the instruction referred to at paragraph 4 herein and jumping vigorously on the trampoline.

(ii) Jumping to an unsafe height, contrary to the said instruction.

(iii) Jumping on the trampoline at the same time as another pupil, thereby adversely affecting the stability of the trampoline and creating, alternatively increasing, the risk that the Plaintiff would lose her balance and fall from the same.

(iv) Failing, in all the circumstances, to have any or any adequate regard for her own safety.

6. Injury, loss and damage whether as alleged at paragraph 5 of the particulars of claim or otherwise are not admitted.

7. It is denied that the Plaintiff's claim qualifies for an award of provisional damages. Without prejudice to the generality of the foregoing denial, in respect of the alleged risk of major reconstruction surgery and disablement the Defendant avers that:

(i) the risk of deterioration is minimal;

(ii) further or alternatively, the deterioration complained of when taken with the Plaintiff's condition as a whole is not serious;

(iii) further or alternatively, the deterioration is a certainty;

(iv) further or alternatively, the current prognosis is insufficiently clear for a proper assessment of the applicability of section 32A of the Supreme Court Act 1981.

8. Further or alternatively, the Defendant will invite the Court to exercise its discretion against making an award of provisional damages.

9. In the premises, it is denied that the Defendant is liable to the Plaintiff, whether as alleged or at all.

Signed

Served *etc*

Example 10

Notice of application seeking declaratory and further relief following refusal of governing body to order stay on ban and fine imposed by disciplinary committee, pending appeal on ground that rules of natural justice were breached

1997 G No 145

IN THE HIGH COURT OF JUSTICE
QUEEN'S BENCH DIVISION

BETWEEN

LAZLO GOULASH

Plaintiff

and

THE NAG RACING ASSOCIATION

Defendant

TAKE NOTICE that the Plaintiff intends to apply to the Judge sitting in chambers in room E101, The Royal Courts of Justice, the Strand, London, on 20 May 1997, at 11.00 am, for an order granting the following relief, namely:

1. A declaration that the Defendant acted unlawfully and in restraint of trade in refusing to stay a penalty imposed on the Plaintiff on 20 May 1997, namely an immediate four-week ban from horse racing, together with a £5,000 fine, pending the resolution of an appeal by the Plaintiff against the said penalty, which appeal is due to be heard by the Defendant's appeals committee on 30 June 1997.

2. Such further or other relief as the Court thinks fit [*i.e. an injunction*].

3. An order that the Defendant do pay the Plaintiff's costs of this application.

The grounds on which this application is made are set out in the affidavit of the Plaintiff sworn on 18 May 1997.

To the Defendant and to its Solicitors, Peace & Makeup, of 3 Bedford Square, London W1.

Dated 18 May 1997

Time estimate for hearing: one hour.

To the Defendant and to its Solicitors, Marple & Poirot, 2 The Village Green, Middle Wallop, Hampshire.

AND TAKE NOTICE that if you do not attend the Court may make such order as it thinks fit.

Example 11

Affidavit in support of interlocutory application in Example 10

> Sworn on behalf of: Plaintiff
> Deponent: L Goulash
> 1st affidavit of Deponent
> Date sworn: 18/5/1997
> Date filed: 18/5/1997

> 1997 G No 145

IN THE HIGH COURT OF JUSTICE
QUEEN'S BENCH DIVISION

BETWEEN

LAZLO GOULASH

Plaintiff

and

THE NAG RACING ASSOCIATION

Defendant

AFFIDAVIT OF LAZLO GOULASH

I, LAZLO GOULASH, of 3 The Gables, Pudding Lane, Lambourn, Berkshire, Professional Jockey, MAKE OATH and say as follows:

1. I am the Plaintiff in these proceedings and make this affidavit in support of my application for an order in the terms of the notice of application herein. The facts and matters to which I depose are all within my personal knowledge and are true.

2. I am a professional jockey and a member of the Defendant Association to whom I pay an annual membership subscription. There is now produced and shown to me and exhibited herewith marked "LG1" a true copy of an agreement between myself and the Defendant dated 13 December 1993 in which I agreed, *inter alia*, to abide by and observe the Defendant's rules and regulations and to be subject to its disciplinary code. [*The existence of a contractual relationship between the plaintiff and the defendant is crucial in order to give rise to a private law action.*]

3. On 30 April 1997 I was booked to ride in five races at Barchester, including the mount of "Ragamuffin" in the 4.20 pm race, the Trollope Stakes. I was drawn with an unfavourable high number which meant that I had a fair amount of ground to make up on those horses which had drawn a low number, nearest the rails. The course has a pronounced camber towards the rails which encourages the field to run towards the inside. This inevitably leads to bunching which is what happened as soon as the race in question started. A number of the horses on my inside moved across much sooner than I had anticipated and I was compelled to follow them. After just one furlong there was a great deal of congestion and I attempted to maintain the straightest possible line down the track. However, horses came up on my inside and four mounts came together. The horse nearest to the rails, "Dobbin", was forced against the rails and panicked, throwing its jockey, Freddie Fox, over the rails.

4. The race continued and I eventually won after a sprint to the line with two other horses. However, the sign went up that a stewards' inquiry was taking place and when I returned to the unsaddling enclosure I was informed that I had been disqualified from the race and reported to the Defendant Association for reckless riding. Shortly afterwards, I received notice to attend a disciplinary hearing at the Defendant's Middle Wallop headquarters. At the hearing, which took place on 20 May 1997, I was not allowed to have legal representation or any other kind of assistance. This placed me at a great disadvantage, since my command of the English language is poor and I found it very difficult to understand what was happening. The evidence against me consisted of a two-page report from the Stewards of the Barchester course. No one attended to give evidence and I was therefore unable to challenge the contents of the report by cross-examining the authors of it.

5. I was then asked if I wanted to say anything on my behalf. I said that I did. The meeting had been televised on Channel 4 and prior to the disciplinary hearing I obtained a video of the race. However, the disciplinary committee would not allow me to play the video, despite the fact that there were video-playing facilities available. Freddie Fox, who was not seriously injured in his fall, attended to give evidence on my behalf but he was left outside in the hallway. I did read a prepared statement to the Committee in

which I set out my version of events. The Chairman of the five-man committee quickly glanced at my statement but did not pass it to any of his colleagues. The whole hearing lasted no more than 10 minutes, following which the committee consulted briefly before announcing that they were imposing a four-week ban on me, together with a £5,000 fine.

6. The consequences of the ban are very serious indeed. First, I am only paid a basic retainer by my Yard and rely heavily on win bonuses to earn a living. As a top rider, the potential earnings are high: last season, when I finished runner-up in the jockeys' championship, I earned, on average, £20,000 per month over the course of the flat season. During the period of my ban, no less than three classic races will be run where the prize money and prestige for winning are very lucrative. One month's ban will also put paid to my chances of winning the jockeys' championship in which I was already well placed. Finally, a finding of liability for a riding accident reflects very badly on a rider and has a detrimental effect on sponsors who, not surprisingly, do not wish to be associated with such incidents. I have already been informed by the garage that loans me a courtesy car that it will be taken away if the ban stands. It is self-evidently clear that if the ban takes effect, I will suffer severe financial hardship.

7. I have submitted an appeal to the Defendant's appeals tribunal which is due to be heard on 30 June 1997. However, by that date, I will have served the ban imposed on me and it will be too late for me to recover the earnings I will inevitably lose during my enforced lay-off. I am advised and believe that the hearing at which the penalty was imposed on me was procedurally unfair and breached the rules of natural justice. I contacted my Solicitors immediately after the hearing and they wrote to the Defendant seeking a stay on the enforcement of the ban and fine pending an appeal. The Defendant has refused that request and there is now produced and shown to me and exhibited herewith marked "LG2" true copies of the relevant correspondence. I would therefore invite the Court to grant me the relief sought to enable me to continue to riding in the meantime.

SWORN

Example 12

Claim by householder in private nuisance for injunction and damages against trustees of unincorporated club arising out of noise and disturbance created by activities of club on nearby go-kart track

Case No EP345987

IN THE EPSOM COUNTY COURT

BETWEEN

CAROLINE MERTON

Plaintiff

and

DAMIAN THRILL and BARRY WALKER
(sued as the trustees of the funds of
THE CARLOS FANDANGO GO-KART CLUB)

Defendant

PARTICULARS OF CLAIM

1. At all material times:

    (i)   the Plaintiff is and was the owner of the property known as "Whiteacre", 15 Oak Hill Drive, Epsom, Surrey; and
    (ii) the Defendants are and were, in common with others, members of the Carlos Fandango Go-Kart Club, an unincorporated club which holds go-kart meetings and races at Pleasant Field, Oak Hill Drive, Epsom, aforesaid (The Field).

2. In their use of The Field, in common with the other members of the said Club, the Defendants have wrongfully caused, permitted and allowed persons to race go-karts, which have made, and continue to make, an unreasonably excessive noise.

PARTICULARS

The Plaintiff moved to her said property in 1995. At the time, the Defendant had a membership of just five people who met to use their go-karts on The Field very infrequently. The go-karts had small engines and made little noise. The Defendant Club gradually grew in size and the meetings took place more frequently. Then, in 1996 The Field was named as a venue for the British go-kart championship, and that summer there was a significant increase in the number of people using the track. From April until September 1996 meetings were held every fortnight and practice sessions were held in between. In addition, the engine capacity of the go-karts increased from 250cc to 500cc. The resultant increase in noise was dramatic and has interfered with the Plaintiff's reasonable enjoyment of her property.

3. By reason of the aforesaid facts and matters, the Plaintiff has been and is being caused nuisance, annoyance and inconvenience, as a consequence whereof the Plaintiff has suffered damage.

4. By letters dated 20 June 1996, 25 July 1996 and 20 September 1996, the Plaintiff wrote to the Defendants asking them to discontinue, alternatively to considerably reduce, their said activities on The Field. The Defendants have failed to respond to any of the Plaintiff's said letters and still continue, and threaten and intend, unless restrained by injunction, to continue the nuisance described in the Particulars to paragraph 2 herein.

5. Further, the Plaintiff is entitled to and claims interest pursuant to section 69 of the County Courts Act 1984 on such damages as are awarded to her, at such rate and for such period as the Court thinks fit.

AND the Plaintiff claims:

(1) An injunction restraining the Defendants, and the members of the Carlos-Fandango Go-Kart Club, from using Pleasant Field, Oak Hill Drive, Epsom, Surrey, for the purposes of go-kart meetings and races, or otherwise.
(2) Damages.
(3) Interest on damages pursuant to section 69 of the County Courts Act 1984.

Signed

Dated *etc*

Example 13

Civil Evidence Act Notice (oral) in claim in Example 12

Case No EP345987

IN THE EPSOM COUNTY COURT

BETWEEN

CAROLINE MERTON

Plaintiff

and

DAMIAN THRILL and BARRY WALKER
(sued as the trustees of the funds of
THE CARLOS FANDANGO GO-KART CLUB)

Defendant

Take notice that at the trial of this action the Plaintiff intends to give in evidence a statement, namely the oral statement of [*identify the maker of the statement; e.g.* Albert Snooks, the former car park attendant of the Carlos Fandango Go-Kart Club], to the effect that:

(a) none of the go-karts which use The Field are fitted with silencers;
(b) planning permission was not obtained by the Defendants to enable The Field to be used for Championship competition;
(c) the local authority regularly monitors the activities of the Carlos Fandango Go-Kart Club and noise levels have exceeded the statutory minimum on three occasions.

And take notice that the relevant particulars of the said statement are as follows, namely that it was made:

(a) by Albert Snooks;
(b) to the Plaintiff's neighbour, Mary Black, of "Blackacre", 17 Oak Hill Drive, Epsom, Surrey;
(c) on 8 July 1996, at about 3.30 pm;
(d) in The Field, as a go-kart meeting was in progress;
(e) in the following circumstances: [*e.g.* as the meeting was in progress, the said Mary Black spoke to the said Albert Snooks about the noise and traffic levels in The Field and he volunteered the above information].

And further take notice that the said Albert Snooks cannot be called as a witness at the trial because he is dead [*or* overseas *or* cannot with reasonable diligence be found *or as the case may be*].

Dated this   day of   1997

Example 14

Civil Evidence Act Notice (document) in Example 12

Case No EP345987

IN THE EPSOM COUNTY COURT

BETWEEN

CAROLINE MERTON

Plaintiff

and

DAMIAN THRILL and BARRY WALKER
(sued as the trustees of the funds of
THE CARLOS FANDANGO GO-KART CLUB)

Defendant

Take notice that at the trial of this action the Defendants desire to give in evidence the statement made in the following document, namely [*identify the document in question, e.g.* the written report of Professor Eddie Speed, a specialist in environmental protection and noise pollution, dated 7 August 1996].

A copy of the said document is attached hereto.

And further take notice that the relevant particulars of the statement are as follows, namely that it was made:

(a) by Professor Eddie Speed;
(b) to [*as appropriate*];
(c) on 7 August 1996;
(d) at his offices in Basingstoke, Hampshire;
(e) in the following circumstances: [*e.g.* Professor Speed was instructed by the Defendants to monitor noise levels during the course of a British go-kart Championship meeting at The Field. He attended on 5 August and carried out the tests referred to in his report, and on which his findings are based].

And further take notice that the said Professor Speed cannot be called as a witness because he is [*e.g.* overseas attending race meetings in his capacity as adviser to the International go-kart Federation, *or as the case may be*].

Dated this   day of   1997

Example 15

Counter-Notice to Civil Evidence Act Notice in Example 14

Case No EP345987

IN THE EPSOM COUNTY COURT

BETWEEN

CAROLINE MERTON

Plaintiff

and

DAMIAN THRILL and BARRY WALKER
(sued as the trustees of the funds of
THE CARLOS FANDANGO GO-KART CLUB)

Defendant

Take notice that the plaintiff requires you to call as a witness at the trial of this action Professor Eddie Speed, particulars of which are set out in your notice dated [*insert*].

And further take notice that the Plaintiff contends that the said Professor Eddie Speed can/should be called as a witness at the trial on the grounds that [*e.g.* that he is ordinarily resident in Basingstoke, and only attends international race meetings abroad at weekends, *or as the case may be*].

Dated this   day of   1997

Useful Names and Addresses

Useful names and addresses of governing bodies and institutions

The Amateur Boxing Association of
  England Limited
Crystal Palace National Sports Centre
Ledrington Road
London SE19
0181 778 0251

Amateur Swimming Association
Crystal Palace National Sports Centre
Ledrington Road
London SE19
0181 778 0131

British Association of Advisers &
  Lecturers in Physical Education
Nelson House
6 The Beacon
Exmouth
Devon EX8 2AG
01395 263247

British Association for Sport and Law
Manchester Metropolitan University
School of Law
Elizabeth Gaskell Campus
Hathersage Road
Manchester M13 0JA

British Athletic Federation
225A Bristol Road
Edgbaston
Birmingham B5 7UB
0121 440 5000

British Boxing Board of Control
1 Calverts Building
London SE1
0171 403 5879

British Judo Association
7a Rutland Street
Leicester
0116 255 9669

British Olympic Association
1 Wandsworth Plain
London SW18
0181 871 2677

Central Council of Physical
  Recreation
Francis House
Francis Street
London SW1
0171 828 3163

Criminal Injuries
Compensation Authority
Morley House
Holborn Viaduct
London EC1
0171 842 6800

FIFA
P.O. Box 85
Hitzigweg 11
Zurich 8030
Switzerland
0041 13849595

FINA
Avenue de Beaumont 9
1012 Lausanne
Switzerland
0041 213126602

Football Association Limited
16 Lancaster Gate
London W2
0171 262 4542

The Football League
Winchester House
Old Marylebone Road
London NW1
0171 224 9944

Football Licensing Authority
Harcourt House
Cavendish Square
London W1
0171 491 7191

The Football Trust
10 Melton Street
London NW1
0171 388 4504

International Amateur Athletic
    Federation (IAAF)
17 Rue Princesse Florestine
MC 980 Monaco
0033 93307070

The Jockey Club
42 Portman Square
London W1
0171 486 4921

National Playing Fields Association
25 Ovington Square
London SW3
0171 584 6445

Rugby Football Union
Twickenham
Middlesex TW1 1 DZ
0181 892 8161

Ski Club of Great Britain
118 Eaton Square
London SW1
0171 245 1033

Sports Council of England
P.O. Box 480
Crystal Palace National Sports Centre
Ledrington Road
London SE19
0181 778 8600

Test & County Cricket Board
Lords Cricket Ground
St. Johns Wood Road
London NW8
0171 286 4405

Index